ESPECIALLY FOR:

_____

FROM:

_____

DATE:

_____

Published by Barbour Books, an imprint of Barbour Publishing, Inc., 1810 Barbour Drive, Uhrichsville, Ohio 44683, www.barbourbooks.com

Our mission is to inspire the world with the life-changing message of the Bible.

Printed in the United States of America.

BIBLE
PRAYERS
FOR
Mothers

BIBLE PRAYERS FOR Mothers

Devotions for the Praying Mom

ED STRAUSS AND JOANNE SIMMONS

BARBOUR BOOKS
An Imprint of Barbour Publishing, Inc.

INTRODUCTION

This book is for mothers like you and contains many ideas to help you pray for your children. In fact, it contains so many suggestions you might feel slightly overwhelmed. But don't worry; you don't need to pray for *all* these things every time you kneel down to intercede for your children. Simply apply the advice that pertains to your children's situation as the need arises and as God's Spirit prompts you. Intercede for your children not only in your daily devotions but throughout the day as God brings them to your mind. Whether you're praying alone or with your husband, we trust this book will give you a clear vision of the effectiveness of a mother's prayers for her children.

We hope you find these readings encouraging. Don't be discouraged if you haven't really been in the habit of praying faithfully for your children until now, because "the LORD's mercies. . .are new every morning" (Lamentations 3:22–23 KJV). You can start praying today, and God will begin to bless your children and transform their lives. And don't give up if your prayers don't seem to be having an immediate effect. Give it time. "Always pray and never give up" (Luke 18:1 NLT).

1.

PRAYING FOR FUTURE CHILDREN

One night four thousand years ago, the sun set over a land on the eastern edge of the Mediterranean. After a day baking under the sun, the rocks were still sweltering with heat, but a wind had just picked up and was soughing in from the sea. In the arid Negev in the south of Canaan, a large shepherds' camp sprawled beneath a star-filled sky, and it was to these tents that God came down.

The Creator of the universe appeared in a vision to a wizened old man named Abraham (then called Abram) and said to him, "Do not be afraid, Abram. I am your shield, your very great reward."

Abraham knew this was so. God had protected him in a recent battle against five foreign armies. But something was weighing on his mind, and, knowing God was near, Abraham took the opportunity to pour out his heart. He was well advanced in years but still childless, so he prayed, "Sovereign LORD, what can you give me since I remain childless and the one who will inherit my estate is Eliezer of Damascus?" Abraham repeated his concern: "You have given me no children; so a servant in my household will be my heir."

But God answered, "This man will not be your heir, but a son who is your own flesh and blood will be your heir." God led Abraham out of his tent, then said, "Look up at the sky and count the stars—if indeed you can count them." Abraham was overwhelmed. There were far, far too many stars to count. Then God said, "So shall your offspring be." Abraham believed the Lord, and God credited it to him as righteousness (Genesis 15:1–6 NIV).

If you're waiting to have children—or to have *more* children—you understand how Abraham felt. Sometimes, although you're thankful that God shields you and blesses you in many ways, and at times you can sense His presence, if you have no children, you still feel incomplete. Or if you're waiting for God to do a desperately needed miracle in one of your children's lives, sometimes you can think of little else.

When God made a promise to Abraham, he believed. Abraham's faith not only made him righteous in God's eyes but ensured that his request would be granted. Sure enough, some years later, his wife, Sarah, became pregnant and gave birth to a son, Isaac (Genesis 21:1–2). Even though it took several years, Abraham "staggered not at the promise of God through unbelief; but was strong in faith" (Romans 4:20 KJV).

Abraham's prayers sprang from his relationship with God. He loved God before anything else, so God was pleased to grant his request. This principle can be true for you too. "Delight yourself also in the LORD, and He shall give you the desires of your heart" (Psalm 37:4 NKJV). "Seek first the kingdom of God and His righteousness, and all these things shall be added to you" (Matthew 6:33 NKJV).

You may not feel that you have a personal relationship with the Lord, however. Maybe you've given little time to prayer and Bible reading down through the years, and though you believe in God, you don't feel close to Him. But you can begin changing all that today. "Let us draw near to God with a sincere heart," we read in

Hebrews 10:22 (NIV). "Draw near to God and He will draw near to you" (James 4:8 NASB).

When you sense that God is present, make the most of the opportunity by praying for your most desperate needs. Often this will mean praying for your children. If you're concerned enough about them to worry about what they're doing or the decisions they're making or the friends they're hanging out with, you should turn those anxious thoughts into prayers.

Even if you don't sense God's presence, rest assured that His eyes are on you and He hears your prayers just the same.

Lord, I thank You that You're always with me and You will never leave me or forsake me. I thank You also for the times You've drawn especially near to me. Thank You for Your holy presence. And thank You for Your promises for me and my children. Lord, please move in my children's lives. Bless them, mold them, and draw them near to You. In Jesus' name I pray. Amen.

FOR FURTHER THOUGHT

- Have you ever felt God's presence? Did you take the opportunity to pray?
- What promises has God made to you regarding your children?
- What promises has God made that He will answer your prayers? Look them up.
- What's a good indication that you should pray for your children?

2.

PROMISES FOR YOUR CHILDREN

As a mother, you often have occasion to pray for your children. They go through many tests in their lives, experience many problems, and sometimes go astray. But on the bright side, often God gives you glimpses of their future greatness. He has destined them to do wonderful things, given them special talents, and calls them into His perfect will. As their mother, you have the privilege of guiding them so that they may rise to fulfill their God-given roles. You are called to pray that they become the men and women of God He intends them to become.

Meditating on God's promises for you and your children will give you the vision, faith, and courage you need to face the future. Life may send so many difficulties your way that you'll be tempted to throw in the towel, but if you know God has a wonderful future in store for you, you'll be encouraged. For example, He promises, "I know the thoughts that I think toward you. . .thoughts of peace and not of evil, to give you a future and a hope" (Jeremiah 29:11 NKJV).

When praying for your children, you can quote God's promises and expect Him to fulfill them. But some of God's promises about Abraham's children were unclear, and he was confused. So he prayed for clarification.

When Abraham first arrived in Canaan, God promised, "To your descendants I will give this land" (Genesis 12:7 NKJV). A couple of years later, He said, "All the land which you see I give to you and your descendants forever"

(Genesis 13:15 NKJV). After a few more years, God said, "I am the LORD, who brought you out of Ur. . .to give you this land to inherit it."

This was the *third* time God had made this promise. Then Abraham prayed, "Lord GOD, how shall I know that I will inherit it?" (Genesis 15:7–8 NKJV). You might reply, "Because God *said* so!" But Abraham wasn't doubting. He just needed clarification. God had promised to give the land to "you and your descendants," so Abraham had the impression that *he* personally would inherit the land and pass it on to his children. But if so, something major needed to happen soon. He wasn't getting any younger.

God then clarified what He meant. He said that Abraham would die and be buried without taking possession of the land. Even Isaac, his miracle son, wouldn't inherit it. "By faith [Abraham] dwelt in the land of promise. . .with Isaac and Jacob, the heirs with him of the same promise" (Hebrews 11:9 NKJV). But after four hundred years Abraham's descendants would return and inherit Canaan (Genesis 15:13, 16).

God makes wonderful promises to you and for your children, and if you're going to bring these promises before Him in prayer, you need to understand them. Only when you know what God's will is can you pray with authority. "If we ask anything according to his will, he hears us. And if we know that he hears us—whatever we ask—we know that we have what we asked of him" (1 John 5:14–15 NIV).

You may protest, "But God hasn't given any promises to *my* children." No? Consider: "Repent, and each of you be baptized in the name of Jesus Christ for the forgiveness of your sins; and you will receive the gift of the Holy Spirit. For the promise is for you and your children" (Acts

2:38–39 NASB). God has promised your children salvation. You definitely can make *that* a matter of prayer.

And God has promised to make your children more Christlike: "He has granted to us His precious and magnificent promises, so that by them you may become partakers of the divine nature" (2 Peter 1:4 NASB). You absolutely can and should pray that your children follow Jesus closely and become godlier as they walk with Him.

> *Dear God, You've made many precious promises to my children and about them. I ask You to fulfill these. You've given each one of my children talents, passions, and dreams, and You have a unique and wonderful future planned for them. Guide them as they grow. Show them the path You'd have them walk, and lead them in Your perfect will. You have promised, "I will not leave you until I have done what I have promised you" (Genesis 28:15 NIV). Fulfill that promise in my children's lives, please. In Jesus' name I pray. Amen.*

FOR FURTHER THOUGHT

- How would clearly understanding God's promises have helped Abraham?
- What specific promises has God made to you for your children?
- How confident are you in praying that God will fulfill these promises?

3.

PRAYING FOR YOUR ISHMAEL

One of the most common pitfalls for mothers—and fathers too—is playing favorites. You may do it without even being aware. For example, if you regularly take your daughter out with you but always leave your son at home, you're being partial. Or if you constantly praise a child who's into sports but show little interest in a child gifted in music or art, you're unwittingly sending a signal that one child pleases you but the others don't meet with your approval.

The most well-known biblical example of playing favorites is found in Isaac and Rebekah. "Isaac loved Esau because he enjoyed eating the wild game Esau brought home, but Rebekah loved Jacob" (Genesis 25:28 NLT). But there is an earlier example of favoritism.

God had promised Abraham a child of his own, but years passed and Sarah became too old to bear children. So she decided to "help" God by giving Abraham her slave girl, Hagar. According to their customs, a child born to Hagar could count as the child of the lawful wife, Sarah. Not long after, Hagar became pregnant and gave birth to a son whom she named Ishmael.

Thirteen more years passed. Then one day God told Abraham, "As for Sarai. . .Sarah shall be her name. I will bless her, and indeed I will give you a son by her" (Genesis 17:15–16 NASB). Now, Abraham fully considered Ishmael his rightful heir and had a great love for him (Genesis 21:10–11). So he prayed, "Oh that Ishmael might live before You!" (Genesis 17:18 NASB). In other words, "Let Ishmael inherit the promises."

God said, "No, but Sarah your wife will bear you a son, and you shall call his name Isaac; and I will establish My covenant with him. . . . As for Ishmael, I have heard you; behold, I will bless him, and will make him fruitful and will multiply him exceedingly" (Genesis 17:19–20 NASB). Ishmael had his place, and "God was with the lad" (Genesis 21:20 KJV), but God had a special calling for Isaac, and Ishmael couldn't crowd him out.

It's only natural that you feel more affection for an especially obedient or talented child, but you must guard against these tendencies. Don't let favoritism creep in. James wrote, "If you favor some people over others, you are committing a sin" (James 2:9 NLT), and that surely applies to children as well as adults.

Very likely you will end up praying more for a willful, disobedient child simply because that child has your attention and needs more prayer. "It is not the healthy who need a doctor, but the sick" (Matthew 9:12 NIV). But even there you must be careful not to give most of your attention to one child. Don't forget to pray for your children who *aren't* experiencing problems at this time. All of your children need spiritual nurturing and daily help from the Spirit of God, and you are responsible for praying that God works in their lives.

God gives each child special gifts. If some of your children don't seem as gifted as others, pray consistently that God will reveal their calling and special abilities. Love them deeply even if they're late bloomers and live for years in the shadow of their more talented brothers and sisters. They need your prayers every bit as much as their more gifted siblings. You may have to make a conscious effort to pray for certain of your children. But it's important that you do. If you don't bless them in prayer, who will?

Heavenly Father, I thank You for each of my children. Forgive me if I have shown favoritism to any of them and neglected others. Forgive me if I have showered one child with attention and affection while failing to let my other children know how deeply I love them. I confess that it's easier to love some children than others, but help me to be a good mother and to model Your love, Your care, and Your favor for all my children. In Jesus' name. Amen.

FOR FURTHER THOUGHT

- Who is your favored child, your "Ishmael"? Why do you favor him/her?

- Do you and your husband favor different children, like Isaac and Rebekah did?

- Do you pray more for one child than another? What can you do to change that?

- Do any of your children feel that they don't meet with your approval?

4.

Boldly Interceding

One day the Lord and two angels in the form of mortals showed up at Abraham's camp beneath the oaks of Mamre. They ate a meal and spoke of Sarah having a child. Then, as they were about to leave, God told Abraham that He was preparing to destroy the wicked cities of the plain, because "the outcry against Sodom and Gomorrah is great" (Genesis 18:20 NKJV). Abraham's nephew Lot and his family lived in Sodom, so Abraham was understandably concerned.

God said the outcry against them was great. Who had been crying out against them if not their victims, living in the same cities? Surely, Abraham reasoned, the victims didn't deserve to be destroyed along with their evil oppressors. So he prayed, "Wilt thou also destroy the righteous with the wicked? . . . Shall not the Judge of all the earth do right?" (Genesis 18:23, 25 KJV). It was a bold approach, but Abraham didn't know what else to say.

It's okay to ask God questions when you sincerely love Him and are merely wondering about something. Abraham asked God how, since He was good and just, He could do such a seemingly unjust thing. He wasn't accusing God of doing wrong. Rather, he was stumped as to why the Lord would do something that seemed to go against His basic nature. So he asked.

God therefore relented. He said if there were fifty righteous people in Sodom, He'd spare the entire city. Abraham then asked God to spare Sodom if only forty-five righteous people were there. God agreed. But Abraham had no peace. So he asked God not to destroy it if it contained only forty godly people. Again, God agreed. Abraham worried that he was pestering the Lord but boldly went on to ask Him to spare the city for the sake of thirty, then twenty, then ten people. God agreed each time.

The next morning, as he watched the thick black smoke churning skyward, Abraham realized that Sodom had been given over *entirely* to evil.

Just the same, Abraham is a tremendous example of intercession. He was moved with compassion and concern and prayed boldly for others, appealing to God's sense of justice and mercy. Many believers are afraid to pray like that. They worry that God will get angry if they pester Him too much. They suspect He will simply shut them out if they don't stop talking.

But God literally commands you not to stop praying to Him for others. The Bible declares, "You who make mention of the Lord, do not keep silent, and give Him no rest till He establishes and till He makes Jerusalem a praise in the earth" (Isaiah 62:6–7 nkjv). Those are strong words: "give Him no rest." You are continually to come boldly before the throne of grace (Hebrews 4:16), without letup, repeating the same requests and not stopping until God takes action and does the necessary miracle.

When praying for your children, you'll discover you often must come before God with the same requests, because your children's basic nature changes slowly, and their issues, problems, and challenges remain fairly constant over time. You'll end up asking God to have mercy on the same faults and sinful tendencies again and again. But do you ever think that God will eventually get tired of hearing you intercede for the same things? You don't *dare* think that. Your children would be in trouble if you ever came to that conclusion.

Whatever your theology on this point, your unceasing love for your children usually wins out, causing you to kneel before God with the same petition, time after time, begging Him to have mercy again. And rest assured: God doesn't get tired of your prayers. You may be weary of praying about the same thing, but God doesn't tire of it. If He *was* prone to despise repetition, He'd have to shut out *most* prayers. But Peter assures us, "The eyes of the LORD are on the righteous, and His ears are open to their prayers" (1 Peter 3:12 NKJV).

Dear God, I hesitate to come before You like Abraham did, repeating his request, insisting that You do what he asked. And I see from this example that it doesn't always work anyway. Yet I know it must be effective sometimes. You do respond to such bold insistence. So help me to have real courage when I present my petitions. In Jesus' name. Amen.

FOR FURTHER THOUGHT

- Does it seem odd that Abraham pleaded again and again with God? Why or why not?

- What requests for your children do you repeatedly bring to God's throne?

- What exactly do you understand Isaiah 62:6–7 to mean?

5.

WHEN YOUR CHILDREN ARE GRIEVING

As a mother, when you see that your son or daughter is going through emotional turmoil, you likely find it difficult to watch them go through a dark valley of grief. Perhaps they've lost their best friend, or are struggling with acceptance, or have been betrayed—and they mope around the house, seemingly inconsolable. No doubt your child's sadness brings out your nurturing nature and makes you want to do what you can to comfort them.

"You know that we dealt with each of you as a father deals with his own children, encouraging, comforting" (1 Thessalonians 2:11–12 NIV). One of the best things you can do is to let your children know by your smiles and hugs that you're there for them. You can speak to them and try to comfort them, but often they don't want to open up about what's troubling them. And they may not be ready to hear advice. But you can always pray.

When Isaac was forty years old, his mother, Sarah, died. Abraham was grief-stricken himself, but Isaac had been very close to his mother and took her death especially hard. Abraham surely prayed for his son when he saw him depressed. And Abraham realized that the solution was a wife. After all, Isaac was forty and unmarried. He had lost his deepest emotional bond and needed a new one. So Abraham summoned his servant, Eliezer, and sent him to Haran. Abraham knew that Isaac would be truly happy only if he married a worshipper of God.

Some time later, Eliezer arrived at a spring outside Haran. He didn't know any of the people in the town and had no idea who would make the best wife for Isaac. But Eliezer had a father's heart, and he knew what to do.

> *"O LORD, God of my master, Abraham," he prayed. "Please give me success today, and show unfailing love to my master, Abraham. See, I am standing here beside this spring, and the young women of the town are coming out to draw water. This is my request. I will ask one of them, 'Please give me a drink from your jug.' If she says, 'Yes, have a drink, and I will water your camels, too!'—let her be the one you have selected as Isaac's wife." (Genesis 24:12–14 NLT)*

Eliezer had arrived with ten camels, so it wasn't likely that anyone would go so far out of her way as to water them all. But a young woman named Rebekah did precisely that! She fulfilled the conditions Eliezer had set, so he knew she was the one. The next day she was already riding south to Canaan, where she married Isaac. "So Isaac was comforted after his mother's death" (Genesis 24:67 NKJV).

You know you should be supportive and help your child make it through a difficult patch, but often you won't know exactly what to do. That's why you must depend on God's direct leading. Know this: God can grant miraculous signs in response to your desperate prayers. "You will seek Me and find Me, when you search for Me with all your heart" (Jeremiah 29:13 NKJV).

You may have to pray desperately for one of your children at times. And God is moved by a mother's sincere prayers. You may feel boxed in with limited options, but

God is not limited. Your hands may be tied, but God is not bound. He can act when things seem hopeless.

Lord, please help me to be sensitive to my children's emotional needs and to be supportive and comforting, not impatient or discouraging. Move my heart to pray desperately for them in their times of need, and please answer mightily. Show me what to do, God. In Jesus' name I pray. Amen.

FOR FURTHER THOUGHT

- How sensitive are you to what your children are going through?
- Do you pray for them when they're struggling with grief or strong emotions?
- Have you ever asked God for a sign to show you His will? What happened?
- When was the last time you prayed desperately for one of your children?

6.

PLEADING WITH THE LORD

At times God requires parents to pray fervently and relentlessly for their families. Isaac was called upon to intercede in that way. "Isaac pleaded [*athar*] with the LORD on behalf of his wife, because she was unable to have children. The LORD answered Isaac's prayer [*athar*], and Rebekah became pregnant with twins" (Genesis 25:21 NLT).

The Hebrew word *athar*, used twice in this verse, means "to entreat abundantly." This was not a brief, one-time prayer. Isaac was pleading with God, and he was pleading abundantly. He poured out his heart again and again for his wife and unborn children, and no doubt he was moved emotionally in the process. Jesus spoke of these kinds of fervent, unceasing prayers when he said that "men always ought to pray and not lose heart" (Luke 18:1 NKJV).

Rebekah herself was driven to prayer over their children. "The children struggled together within her; and she said, 'If all is well, why am I like this?' So she went to inquire of the LORD. And the LORD said to her: 'Two nations are in your womb, two peoples shall be separated from your body; one people shall be stronger than the other, and the older shall serve the younger' " (Genesis 25:22–23 NKJV).

The Bible gives us the exact wording of Rebekah's prayer but not Isaac's. Why? Probably because Isaac's "abundant" prayers were so long and so frequent. Most people's attention is drawn to Rebekah's question, but without Isaac's passionate *athar*, there would have been nothing for her to ask the Lord about.

Isaiah lamented, "There is no one who calls on Your name, who stirs himself up to take hold of You" (Isaiah 64:7 NKJV). Let's face it: many people are somewhat apathetic when it comes to prayer. They either don't believe in its power or aren't concerned enough to seek God. So they just rock along and trust that a bad situation will get better of its own accord, over time.

It took twenty years for Isaac to clue in to the need to pray—*really* pray (compare Genesis 25:20 and 25:26). Very likely, he had said small prayers over the years, but nothing worked until he set himself to pray like a house on fire. Maybe he prayed this way because Rebekah had become miserable. Like her daughter-in-law Rachel after her, Rebekah probably said words to the effect of, "Give me children, or else I die!" (Genesis 30:1 NKJV).

Sometimes your children may be involved in bad behavior, and God has no choice but to allow them to suffer punishment. The protective wall that normally surrounds them has been breached, and a gap has opened up. But God says, "I searched for a man among them who would build up the wall and stand in the gap before Me for the land, so that I would not destroy it" (Ezekiel 22:30 NASB). At such times, His Spirit seeks to move the hearts of mothers so they will "stand in the gap" and pray for their families.

Many modern women don't usually pray fervently for their husbands or their families. It's hard work. You have to wake yourself up, shake off the lethargy, and incite yourself to action. You have to get ahold of God like Jacob did when he frantically, desperately wrestled the Angel of the Lord and refused to let go until he received the blessing (Genesis 32:24–28).

God promises, "You will seek Me and find Me, when you search for Me with *all your heart*" (Jeremiah 29:13 NKJV, emphasis added). "Let us therefore come boldly unto the throne of grace, that we may obtain mercy, and find grace to help in time of need" (Hebrews 4:16 KJV). Notice this verse says "in time of need." You won't have to pray so hard *most* of the time. Just in times of special need.

Dear God, help me to pray fervently, that I might receive Your help in this time of need. Forgive me for being apathetic when it comes to prayer. Fill me with Your Holy Spirit, because You said that "the Spirit Himself makes intercession for us with groanings which cannot be uttered" (Romans 8:26 NKJV). Holy Spirit, please stir my heart! Help me to be moved mightily to pray about pressing needs and desperate situations. Help me to "stand in the gap" in prayer. Motivate me to come boldly before Your throne of grace. In Jesus' name I pray. Amen.

FOR FURTHER THOUGHT

- What do you think Isaac's impassioned prayers sounded like?
- Why do many women not really spend time in fervent prayer?
- When have you been moved to pray an *athar* prayer?
- How has God answered when you've prayed with all your heart?

7.

PRAYING THE BIG PICTURE

Jacob had deviously obtained the birthright and the blessing from his brother, and now Esau wanted to kill him. Rebecca therefore persuaded Isaac to send Jacob to Haran "to find a wife." That *was* a secondary motive, but her primary reason was to get him out of danger.

Isaac now recognized Jacob as his heir, so with his eyes on the big picture, he gave him this parting blessing: "May God Almighty bless you, and make you fruitful and multiply you, that you may be an assembly of peoples; and give you the blessing of Abraham, to you and your descendants with you, that you may inherit the land" (Genesis 28:3–4 NKJV).

As Jacob slept beside the road a couple of nights later, God appeared in a dream and said, "I am the LORD God of Abraham your father and the God of Isaac; the land on which you lie I will give to you and your descendants. . . . Behold, I am with you and will keep you wherever you go, and will bring you back to this land; for I will not leave you until I have done what I have spoken to you" (Genesis 28:13, 15 NKJV).

What promises! God spoke of Jacob's amazing destiny—a multitude of descendants who would inherit all of Canaan. But Jacob's focus was far smaller: all he could think about was being safe, having food, staying warm, and making it back home again. He responded, "If God will be with me, and keep me in this way that I am going, and give me bread to eat and clothing to put on, so that I come back to my father's house in peace, then the LORD shall be my God" (Genesis 28:20–21 NKJV).

God had said His presence would never leave Jacob. He promised to bless him with descendants who would fill the land. The all-powerful God would certainly keep Jacob alive to ensure that this tremendous future happened. That was a given. But many believers can sympathize with Jacob's concerns. Often they too get their eyes off God's promises for their lives and become anxious. Sometimes all they can think about is how they're going to pay their bills or survive some crisis.

Sometimes you might relate to your children with the same out-of-focus attitude: all you can see are their present pressing needs and problems and you lack the long-term vision of the man or woman of God they're destined to become. While it's true that you should enjoy your children where they're at and not expect too much of them in their current stage, it's important to keep God's purposes for their lives in mind. They won't remain children forever.

To Jacob, God's promises about "descendants" were indefinite uncertainties—after all, he didn't even have a wife yet. But God was speaking about real people, starting with his twelve sons and several daughters (Genesis 37:35). God said, "The land on which you lie I will give to you and your descendants." This was a very concrete promise.

Solomon said, "Where there is no vision, the people perish" (Proverbs 29:18 KJV). Had Jacob focused on God's promises and mulled over them, they would have set ablaze a vision in his imagination—a vision that would've given him hope and sustained him during difficult times. God had a wonderful future for Jacob and his children.

But Jacob wasn't thinking about his children. . .yet.

You today also do well to remember God's promises: " 'For I know the plans I have for you,' declares the LORD, 'plans to prosper you and not to harm you, plans to give you hope and a future' " (Jeremiah 29:11 NIV). And that future includes God's blessings on your children.

Father, You have wonderful things planned for my children, things I can't even imagine right now. But You've given me hints and glimpses of their future so that I can pray for them and help prepare them for what's coming. You've also ordained these visions of the future to give me hope and to breathe endurance into my bones, because some days are going to be very difficult. Help me to accept Your encouragement. In the name of Your Son, Jesus, I pray. Amen.

FOR FURTHER THOUGHT

- When do *you* miss the big picture and focus on your present problems?
- Why did Jacob not think much of what God had planned for his children?
- Why is it important for God's people to have a vision for the future?

8.

CLAIMING PROMISES OF PROTECTION

Nothing is quite as chilling as realizing that your children's lives are in danger and that the situation is completely out of your hands and beyond your control. If nothing else will drive you into the presence of God, surely this will do it. It could be a sudden, terrifying accident or the dull, ongoing threat of bullying, but in whatever form it comes, maybe you can't do much about it or have no clear idea what to do. So you turn to the Lord in prayer.

Twenty-one years had passed since a frightened Jacob fled north from Canaan, fearing for his life, uncertain of God's love and care. He had endured many hardships in those two decades and had spent countless nights alone, awake, watching over flocks of sheep. All this had drawn him close to the Lord.

He was now headed back to his homeland, Canaan. With him were his four wives, eleven children, and vast flocks and herds. He sent messengers to inform his brother, Esau, that he was coming. He reasoned it was better to tell him up front than for Esau to learn that he had tried to sneak back into Canaan quietly. That wouldn't work and would only serve to anger Esau. But when Jacob's messengers returned, they brought alarming news: Esau not only was riding to meet him but was bringing four hundred armed men!

Jacob was understandably afraid. But his prayer shows how much he had matured and what a deep relationship with God he had gained. He was now a spiritual man who viewed his problems in the light of God's promises. He prayed:

> "O God of my father Abraham and God of my father Isaac, O LORD, who said to me, 'Return to your country and to your relatives, and I will prosper you,' I am unworthy of all the loving-kindness and of all the faithfulness which You have shown. . . . Deliver me, I pray, from the hand of my brother, from the hand of Esau; for I fear him, that he will come and attack me and the mothers with the children. For You said, 'I will surely prosper you and make your descendants as the sand of the sea, which is too great to be numbered.' " (Genesis 32:9–12 NASB)

What a difference in his prayers! Jacob sandwiched his request for protection between two of God's promises—promises that he now quoted. Jacob was declaring, "This is Your Word, Lord. I'm trusting You to fulfill it and to protect me and mine."

Jacob was afraid, yes, but he reasoned that if God said, "Return to your country and to your relatives, and I will prosper you," then He wasn't sending him back to be killed. For God to prosper him, He had to keep him alive. And when praying for God to protect his children, Jacob declared, "For You said, 'I will surely prosper you and make your descendants. . .too great to be numbered.' " Jacob reasoned that for this promise to be fulfilled, God had to keep his children safe.

Again, Jacob's remembrance of God's promises didn't mean he experienced no fear but that he was determined to trust God despite his fear.

The wonderful news is that when he saw Jacob the next day, "Esau ran to meet him and embraced him, threw his arms around his neck, and kissed him. And they both wept" (Genesis 33:4 NLT). Nobody died that day.

Quoting God's Word is an integral part of effective prayer. Moses reminded God of His promises when he prayed (Exodus 32:12–14). So did King Solomon (1 Kings 8:28–30). So did Jehoshaphat (2 Chronicles 20:5–9). And Jesus repeatedly quoted the Word when resisting the devil (Matthew 4:1–11). If you wish to be certain that God hears your prayers, make petitions backed up by God's promises.

Father in heaven, You are my Protector, my high Rock where I take refuge in times of danger. You are my Fortress from the enemy. You have given many promises in Your Word that You will protect me and my family. I ask You now to rise up and drive off the enemy before us and behind us. Protect my children when I can't be there to take care of them. Put Your angels around them to keep them safe. Nullify any threat against them. In Jesus' name I pray. Amen.

FOR FURTHER THOUGHT

- Has your prayer life matured over the years? How has hardship strengthened it?
- What kind of prayers do you pray when your children are in danger?
- What promises from scripture do you claim when you pray?
- How has God answered your prayers for your children's protection?

9.

INTERCEDING FOR YOUR CHILDREN

Job had ten children, and he often interceded for them—not just when they were little but also after they were grown and lived in their own homes.

> *In the land of Uz there lived a man whose name was Job. This man was blameless and upright; he feared God and shunned evil. He had seven sons and three daughters. . . . His sons used to hold feasts in their homes on their birthdays, and they would invite their three sisters to eat and drink with them. When a period of feasting had run its course, Job would make arrangements for them to be purified. Early in the morning he would sacrifice a burnt offering for each of them, thinking, "Perhaps my children have sinned and cursed God in their hearts." This was Job's regular custom. (Job 1:1–5 NIV)*

About these burnt offerings: sacrifices to God were never made without prayer. They were performed with intercession invoking God's mercy and with prayers of blessing and gratitude. We have ample testimony that Job prayed. The book of Job is filled with his prayers, complaints, questions, protests, confessions, and praises to God.

You might wonder if Job's prayers for his children were a failure, since, after all, God took their lives. But there is no record of Job praying for God to bless his sons and daughters with long lives, abundant possessions, or worldly happiness. Job's family enjoyed great riches, so he was on guard against an attitude of selfish privilege in his children. He was concerned with their spiritual state.

Job's concern was that perhaps his children had "cursed God *in their hearts*." He said, "If I have made gold my hope, or said to fine gold, 'You are my confidence'; if I have rejoiced because my wealth was great, and because my hand had gained much. . .this also would be an iniquity deserving of judgment, for I would have denied God who is above" (Job 31:24–25, 28 NKJV). Agur also described this attitude when he prayed, "Give me neither poverty nor riches. . .that I not be full and deny You and say, 'Who is the LORD?' " (Proverbs 30:8–9 NASB).

The lives of Job's children were cut short in truly exceptional circumstances—to test Job's faith in an unprecedented manner—but God nevertheless honored Job's prayers to keep his children in right standing, and there is no valid reason to doubt that He received them into paradise.

As a mother, you want your children's physical needs to be met. That's why you go to work every day. You want your children to get a good education and to have every advantage and to succeed in this world. But that's also the desire of the ungodly, of "men of the world, whose portion is in this life. . . . They are satisfied with children, and leave their abundance to their babes" (Psalm 17:14 NASB).

But there is a much more important aspect of your children's lives that you must not ignore. John gave the correct priorities when he said, "I pray that in all respects you may prosper and be in good health, *just as* your soul prospers" (3 John 1:2 NASB, emphasis added). It's not wrong to prosper materially, so long as you and your children understand that "one's life does not consist in the abundance of the things he possesses" (Luke 12:15 NKJV).

But, as Job's concerns show, we can't take it for granted that our children are learning this truth and won't slip up. The happy little lessons your children get in Sunday school aren't enough, nor do the quarters you may give them to drop into the offering complete their spiritual education. You must model godly behavior yourself and then constantly pray for opportunities to underline spiritual values for your children.

Dear Father in heaven, please help me to focus on what is truly important in my children's lives. Help this right focus to be reflected in my prayers for them. Help me to model an appreciation of spiritual priorities in my own life and daily conversation. And please help my children to gain a clear understanding of the importance of spiritual blessings, good character, loving behavior, and honest lives. In Jesus' name I pray. Amen.

FOR FURTHER THOUGHT

- What kinds of blessings do you continually pray for your children to receive?

- How important is it that God keeps your children close to Him?

- Do your children understand the importance of spiritual things?

- What can you do or say to impress spiritual principles on your children?

10.

PRAYER BEFORE A SERIOUS TALK

You frequently hear people say that prayer is "talking with God," but most of us will never have a conversation with God like Moses had. When he approached the burning bush,

> *God called to him from the middle of the bush, "Moses! Moses!" "Here I am!" Moses replied. . . . Then the LORD told him, "I have certainly seen the oppression of my people in Egypt. . . . Now go, for I am sending you to Pharaoh. You must lead my people Israel out of Egypt." But Moses protested to God, "Who am I to appear before Pharaoh? Who am I to lead the people of Israel out of Egypt?" God answered, "I will be with you."* (Exodus 3:4, 7, 10–12 NLT)

Then Moses questioned, "If I go to the people of Israel and tell them, 'The God of your ancestors has sent me to you,' they will ask me, 'What is his name?' Then what should I tell them?" (3:13 NLT). Moses raised more objections: "What if they won't believe me or listen to me? What if they say, 'The LORD never appeared to you'?" (4:1 NLT). Each time, God patiently answered Moses' questions.

Then Moses tried getting out of the job. He argued, "O Lord, I'm not very good with words. I never have been, and I'm not now, even though you have spoken to me. I get tongue-tied, and my words get tangled." But God ordered, "Now go! I will be with you as you speak, and

I will instruct you in what to say" (4:10, 12 NLT). Moses blurted out, "Lord, please! Send anyone else" (4:13 NLT). However, God had anticipated Moses' reluctance and informed him that his brother, Aaron, was already on his way to join him.

How much better to have Isaiah's attitude: when God asked, "Whom should I send as a messenger to this people? Who will go for us?" Isaiah said, "Here I am. Send me" (Isaiah 6:8 NLT). Moses *also* first answered, "Here I am," but instead of saying, "Send me," he said, "Send anyone else."

Although you may not be crazy about it, often your pillow talk with your husband will be about your children's misbehavior. It's not exactly the kind of thing you want to discuss just before going to sleep. But the conversation eventually comes down to this: "We need to talk with them." Now, unless you enjoy butting heads with a willful child or a sullen teen, you understand how Moses felt.

Later, you complain to God, "How can we speak with them? We don't have all the facts, we don't know what they're going through that they're not telling us, and from experience we know they may not be very receptive. Then we'll have to lay down the law, and we'll be either too harsh or too easy on them." But God's answer is: "I will be with you." You may argue, "I'm not very good with words," but God's answer is: "I will instruct you in what to say."

Obviously, at times like this, you need to pray and ask God for help and wisdom. He knows what your children are going through, and He knows what it takes to get through to them. He can certainly instruct you in what to tell them. He can help you decide on the appropriate discipline, if needed. And, very importantly, He can help you "speak the truth in love" (Ephesians 4:15 NLT).

The good news is, if you sincerely pray before you speak with your children, as Jesus promised, "It is not you who will be speaking—it will be the Spirit of your Father speaking through you" (Matthew 10:20 NLT).

Lord, forgive me for my objections and excuses; You know I don't relish trying to balance discipline with sensitivity to where my kids are at. I don't always enjoy "talking" with my kids because often they aren't receptive. But I look to You, Lord, and trust You to help me overcome my feelings of inadequacy. Be with me now as I go to speak with them, and help my words to have a good effect. In Jesus' name I pray. Amen.

FOR FURTHER THOUGHT

- How closely do you identify with Moses when you need to talk to your kids about their behavior?
- Why can correcting your children still be unpleasant even when God helps you?
- How can prayer help you overcome your reluctance?

11.

POWERFUL PRAYERS OF PRAISE

Sometimes it's easy to get the idea that prayer is basically asking God for things, petitioning Him for serious requests, or interceding for others. But above all, prayer is communication with the Lord, and at times you need to express your awe and gratitude to Him. In the Bible, expressions of thankfulness often took the form of songs praising God for His mighty acts. "Sing a new song to the LORD, for he has done wonderful deeds. His right hand has won a mighty victory; his holy arm has shown his saving power!" (Psalm 98:1 NLT).

The earliest prayer extolling God's mighty acts in the Bible is the Song of Moses, composed immediately after God engulfed the Egyptians in the Red Sea (Exodus 15:1–18). Here are some highlights from it:

> *"Your right hand, LORD, was majestic in power.*
> *Your right hand, LORD, shattered the enemy.*
> *"In the greatness of your majesty you threw*
> *down those who opposed you. You unleashed your*
> *burning anger; it consumed them like stubble.*
> *By the blast of your nostrils the waters piled up.*
> *The surging waters stood up like a wall; the deep*
> *waters congealed in the heart of the sea. The enemy*
> *boasted, 'I will pursue, I will overtake them.' . . .*
> *But you blew with your breath, and the sea covered*
> *them. They sank like lead in the mighty waters.*

Who among the gods is like you, LORD? Who is like you—majestic in holiness, awesome in glory, working wonders?

"You stretch out your right hand, and the earth swallows your enemies. In your unfailing love you will lead the people you have redeemed. In your strength you will guide them to your holy dwelling."
(Exodus 15:6–13 NIV)

Moses' heart was overflowing with awe and excitement at the tremendous miracle God had just done, and this song burst forth spontaneously. He was singing a prayer to God, and because his words were set to music, the entire nation was able to join in.

Paul encouraged Christians to constantly sing God's praises as well, "speaking to yourselves in psalms and hymns and spiritual songs, singing and making melody in your heart to the Lord" (Ephesians 5:19 KJV). Not only does God appreciate your sincere praise—including songs of joy and thanksgiving—but it inspires and strengthens your own spirit. These are two excellent reasons for you to thank God when He gains victories in your children's lives.

They need not be major accomplishments, either. You can thank God for the many small victories. Your children are delighted with small triumphs, and you can be too. "Give thanks for *everything* to God the Father" (Ephesians 5:20 NLT, emphasis added). An old song urges, "Count your blessings, name them one by one. Count your many blessings, see what God has done." For example, you can thank God that your daughter made a new friend today or that your son excelled on the sports field.

Beyond just specific accomplishments, you can praise God for ongoing gifts—such as blessing your daughter with a sweet, helpful spirit, or endowing your son with computer skills. If you determine to have a grateful attitude, you'll quickly realize how much you have to be glad about. Your thanks will continually trickle out in happy, victorious expressions of faith and overflow into your whole life.

Even if you can't readily think of any *new* things God has done in your children's lives, you can praise Him for the fact that they're continually spared misfortune and that they are, for the most part, healthy.

Choosing to have a thankful attitude can increase your faith too. If you're constantly giving God thanks for the many small miracles He has done, you're reminded daily of His power. You're also reminded of His love and concern as you realize how active He is in your life and in your children's lives.

Dear God, with all the minor worries and challenges and more pressing problems my children face, I often forget to thank You for the many, many good things You're doing in their lives and for the numerous victories You bring about. Forgive me for taking these for granted. Fill my heart with gratitude and my lips with praise. Help me to count the many blessings You give to my children. In Jesus' name I pray. Amen.

FOR FURTHER THOUGHT

- How often do you thank God for doing good things in your children's lives?
- What has God done this week for which you can express gratitude?
- How can a thankful attitude increase your faith?

12.

TURNING ON THE TAP

When your kids are hot, fussy, hungry, thirsty, or out of patience, they'll most likely blame you for the situation, or for not being able to fix it. Most frequently this happens when they're sick, when they've misplaced something, or when the air conditioner isn't working.

The Israelites often blamed Moses. God was constantly present in the pillar of cloud and fire, and this cloud led the Israelites in all their travels (Exodus 13:21–22; 40:36–37). After they crossed the Red Sea, His cloud guided them south and stopped at a place called Rephidim, beside Mount Sinai (Horeb). There was only one problem: there was no water there.

Frustrated, the Israelites accused Moses of making a mistake in leading them to this place. But Moses was only following the cloud. The people then started quarreling. They demanded, "Is the LORD among us or not?" Now, they could see the cloud. God clearly *was* among them. What they actually were saying was that if God cared for them, He should provide water. Doubting that He would, however, they took out their frustrations on Moses, insisting, "Give us water to drink."

Moses replied, "Why do you quarrel with me? Why do you put the LORD to the test?" The Israelites then began accusing, "Why did you bring us up out of Egypt to make us. . .die of thirst?" Imagine: accusing God of pretending to deliver them but actually only leading them out into the desert to kill them all with thirst.

Moses went aside and cried out to God, "What am I to do with these people? They are almost ready to stone me." He had the right idea to get away and pray, but his prayer was off target. He didn't expect God to provide water. All he wanted was an effective method of crowd control. . .until they could move to someplace that did have water.

But God answered, "Take in your hand the staff with which you struck the Nile, and go. I will stand there before you by the rock at Horeb. Strike the rock, and water will come out of it for the people to drink" (Exodus 17:1–7 NIV). So Moses struck the rock and water flowed out.

Now, abundant water had been near the surface the entire time, ready to burst out. It had been there for thousands of years. They just needed to turn on the tap, so to speak. God knew how He was going to provide water for them before they ever arrived in Rephidim. In fact, He had given thought to the Israelites' need before time began. Yet He didn't reveal His tender care until they were nearly wild with thirst. Often God lets you be tested before He does a miracle. Such tests have a way of revealing what's in your heart.

You have to be in the place God has appointed you to be before He can do a miracle. Abraham had to be on Mount Moriah, prepared to sacrifice Isaac, before God provided a ram. That's why the proverb says, "On the mountain of the LORD it will be provided" (Genesis 22:14 NIV). If you're serving God, He will come through for you.

Moses called the place Meribah ("quarreling") because the Israelites quarreled with him there. He also called it Massah ("testing") because they tested the Lord. The people had their eyes completely off God's love. But Moses didn't understand either, as his prayer revealed. You have to grasp the truth that God is your loving heavenly Father and delights in providing for you and your children. And many times, your prayers simply turn on the tap.

Father in heaven, sometimes I struggle to believe that You care about me and my children, particularly when we go through severe tests that nearly convince me You aren't concerned at all. Help me to remember that You truly do care and that Your ears are wide open to my prayers. It may take a little effort on my part at times—striking a rock—but You delight to provide. Thank You for thinking of me and my children even before time began. Thank You for caring for us. In Jesus' name I pray. Amen.

FOR FURTHER THOUGHT

- What are some times your children have complained and blamed you?
- Has God done any miracles for you similar to His supplying water for the people of Israel?
- Do you believe that God actually delights in providing for your family?

13.

Moses' Compassionate Intercession

Even young children can be willful, but as a general rule, kids enter their most rebellious stage during their teen years, when they often openly question or reject what their parents have taught them. Other times, they maintain a Christian facade but backslide in their hearts. Often this abandoning of moral restraint is eventually followed by an unspiritual lifestyle.

When Moses was on Mount Sinai speaking with God, the Israelites camping at the bottom of the mountain "quickly turned aside from the way which [He] commanded them" (Exodus 32:8 NASB). They made a golden calf and began to worship it with wild music and lascivious dancing. God was so furious that He said to Moses, "Let Me alone, that My wrath may burn hot against them and I may consume them. And I will make of you a great nation."

But Moses prayed, "LORD, why does Your wrath burn hot against Your people whom You have brought out of the land of Egypt with great power and with a mighty hand? Why should the Egyptians. . .say, 'He brought them out to harm them, to kill them in the mountains, and to consume them from the face of the earth'? Turn from Your fierce wrath, and relent from this harm to Your people" (Exodus 32:10–13 NKJV).

So the Lord relented. But He still intended to punish the Israelites, so the next day Moses prayed, "Oh, these people have committed a great sin, and have made for themselves a god of gold! Yet now, if You will forgive their sin—but if not, I pray, blot me out of Your book which You have written" (Exodus 32:31–32 NKJV).

What can possibly explain Moses' strong protective attitude? Love. Moses had tender compassion for the Israelites.

Despite the fact that they had given in to such carnal lusts and idolatry, Moses cared deeply for the people and his heart went out to them—just as you, as a mother, feel pangs of compassion for wayward children. From the onset, Moses had felt God telling him, "Carry them in your bosom as a nurse carries a nursing infant" (Numbers 11:12 NASB). Paul wrote, "We proved to be gentle among you, as a nursing mother tenderly cares for her own children" (1 Thessalonians 2:7 NASB).

At the moment, however, God was angry with the rebels. He had a deep love for Moses and wouldn't consider destroying him, so He insisted that He would only punish the guilty. Because of Moses' prayer, however, God said He wouldn't wipe out the Israelites—*now*. But He warned that He would eventually punish them. Plus He sent a plague that very day that slew the guiltiest individuals (Exodus 32:35).

Moses knew the Israelites had sinned seriously and deserved to be punished, so he put his own life on the line when pleading for mercy for them. He not only reasoned with God (32:11–12) but reminded Him of His promises (32:13). These were powerful prayers. Not even Moses could completely shield the Israelites from God's wrath, but his prayers did save the nation from being wiped out.

Have you ever felt a strong protective instinct toward your disobedient children? Although you know they've sinned, you desire to shield them from the worst of the consequences. God still seeks bold, selfless intercessors today. He says, "I sought for a man among them who would. . .stand in the gap before Me on behalf of the land, that I should not destroy it" (Ezekiel 22:30 NKJV). Will you intercede?

> *Dear God, I thank You for my children, even when they're willfully disobedient. They're mine, flaws and all. Lord, I've tried to teach them Your ways, but sometimes they've turned away. You gave them to me, and You gave me love for them, so I feel pain when they suffer for their disobedience. I ask You, even if You must chastise them to teach them important lessons, to remember that they're Your children too, and "in wrath remember mercy" (Habakkuk 3:2 KJV). They are the work of Your hands. Let Your tender mercies be over all Your works (Psalm 145:9). In Jesus' name. Amen.*

FOR FURTHER THOUGHT

- What kinds of strong emotions do you feel for your children?
- Are you often gentle with your kids?
- Have you ever prayed for God to have mercy on your disobedient children?

14.

PRAYING TO SEE GOD'S BEAUTY

When your children are little, they readily grasp the basic Gospel message that "God is love" (1 John 4:8 KJV) and that "God so loved the world that he gave his one and only Son, that whoever believes in him shall not perish but have eternal life" (John 3:16 NIV). They believe Jesus is good and, as the Bible says, that He "went around doing good" (Acts 10:38 NIV). And they know Jesus loves *them*.

These simple messages resonate powerfully with young children. As a result, they think of God primarily as good and find the Gospel appealing. But as they grow older, friends, sports, video games, the opposite sex, and many other things fill their thoughts. And as they experience pain, suffering, and disappointment, they may begin doubting that God is so wonderful after all.

As your children grow, and especially as they enter their teen years, you'll find yourself praying that they will walk in the truth and "worship the LORD in the beauty of holiness" (1 Chronicles 16:29 KJV). You'll want their hearts to be captivated by the beauty of God, and you'll want them to rediscover that Jesus is "altogether lovely" (Song of Solomon 5:16 KJV).

One day God told Moses, "You have found favor in My sight and I have known you by name." God loved Moses, and Moses loved Him in return. His heart was filled with longing to see God's radiant splendor, so he said, "I pray You, show me Your glory!"

God replied, "I Myself will make all My goodness pass

before you, and will proclaim the name of the LORD before you." But He added, "You cannot see My face, for no man can see Me and live!" Then He said, "Behold, there is a place by Me, and you shall stand there on the rock; and it will come about, while My glory is passing by, that I will put you in the cleft of the rock and cover you with My hand until I have passed by. Then I will take My hand away and you shall see My back, but My face shall not be seen" (Exodus 33:17–23 NASB).

Many believers since then have longed to see God. David prayed, "One thing have I desired of the LORD, that will I seek after; that I may dwell in the house of the LORD all the days of my life, to behold the beauty of the LORD" (Psalm 27:4 KJV). On earth, even Moses couldn't look directly upon God's face, but in heaven everyone will see it. "His servants shall serve him: and they shall see his face" (Revelation 22:3–4 KJV).

Even now, in direct proportion to how desperately they seek God's presence, Christians can drink in increasing levels of His glory, and it will transform them. "We all, who with unveiled faces contemplate the Lord's glory, are being transformed into his image with ever-increasing glory" (2 Corinthians 3:18 NIV). So we pray, "Let the beauty of the LORD our God be upon us" (Psalm 90:17 KJV).

How do you behold God's beauty? By faithfully reading God's Word, seeking to know Him through prayer, and asking Him to fill your heart and transform your life. The psalmist wrote, "I will meditate on the glorious splendor of Your majesty, and on Your wondrous works" (Psalm 145:5 NKJV).

Another psalm entreats God, "May your deeds be shown to your servants, your splendor to their children"

(Psalm 90:16 NIV). Your children naturally look to you as an example of God's nature and love. If what they see in your life is attractive, they'll find the God you tell them about to be appealing as well. And as they grow older, make their faith their own, and develop a loving relationship with Him, the beauty of the Lord will be upon their lives as well.

Dear Father, help my children to know that You love them immensely, more than words can say. Restore their faith that "You are good, and do good" (Psalm 119:68 NKJV) and that they can trust You entirely. I pray that they will thirst for Your presence, find You, and drink deeply of You. Fill them with Your Holy Spirit, and let Your radiant presence overflow within them and be upon every aspect of their lives. In Jesus' name I pray. Amen.

FOR FURTHER THOUGHT

- Why are young children so attracted to God and to His Son, Jesus?

- Do you personally long to know God and enter into His presence?

- How can you make this your prayer for your children?

- How does the beauty of God come into your children's lives?

15.

PRAYING THE PRIESTLY BLESSING

In ancient Israel, people greeted one another by blessing each other in the name of the Lord. "Boaz came from Bethlehem, and said to the reapers, 'The LORD be with you!' And they answered him, 'The LORD bless you!'" (Ruth 2:4 NKJV). A more formal, more intentional blessing is found in the Psalms: "The blessing of the LORD be upon you; we bless you in the name of the LORD!" (Psalm 129:8 NKJV).

Whenever you see the phrase "the LORD" in the Bible in small caps, it's a substitute for the name of God, Yahweh. The name of Yahweh is found everywhere in the Old Testament, but when reading the scriptures aloud, the Jews in New Testament times considered God's name so sacred that they didn't pronounce it; instead they substituted "the LORD." So when translating the scriptures into English, the translators simply wrote "the LORD."

Besides the above blessings, a beautiful benediction is found in the Law of Moses. The Lord told Moses to instruct Aaron and his sons: "This is how you are to bless the Israelites. Say to them: 'The LORD bless you and keep you; the LORD make his face shine on you and be gracious to you; the LORD turn his face toward you and give you peace'" (Numbers 6:22–26 NIV). God added, "So they will put my name on the Israelites, and I will bless them" (v. 27 NIV).

Let's take a closer look and consider how you as a mother can richly bless your children: "This is how you are to bless the Israelites." You want to know how to truly bless your kids? This is how to do it! Often, however, people repeat this blessing quickly, basking in its transcendent beauty but not meditating on the words or fully comprehending their meaning. So say it with meaning.

When uttering the phrase, "The LORD bless you and keep you," you're asking God to act in abundant goodness toward your children and to supply all their needs, spiritual and physical. You're praying that He will guard them from evil, accidents, and disease. Of course, as a mother, you desire all these things for them.

In praying, "The LORD turn his face toward you," and "The LORD make his face shine on you," you're praying for Him to be intimately involved in their lives, to turn and gaze with love and favor upon them, and to hear and answer their prayers. The imagery here is beautiful, and God really does do these things when you bless your children.

Finally, in praying, "The LORD. . .be gracious to you. . .and give you peace," you're asking God to look on your kids with grace and forgiveness, which brings peace. You're also praying for them to be aware of God's love and power, because Isaiah 26:3 (NKJV) says, "You will keep him in perfect peace, whose mind is stayed on You, because he trusts in You." Isaiah also promises regarding your children: "Great will be their peace" (Isaiah 54:13 NIV).

And God made a promise concerning this benediction: "So they will put my name on the Israelites, and I *will* bless them" (emphasis added). So be careful: you are not to pray such blessings upon evildoers (2 John 1:10–11). To pray, "The LORD bless you," is to invoke the name Yahweh upon someone, and His name only truly marks those who are His saved children. When speaking of heaven, John wrote, "His servants. . .shall see His face, and His name shall be on their foreheads" (Revelation 22:3–4 NKJV).

In heaven, your children will enjoy the fullness of God's presence and blessing eternally. But God wants them to enjoy a good measure of it now.

Lord, I thank You from the bottom of my heart that You richly bless me and my family. Thank You that You indeed turn toward me and my children and make Your radiant, glorious face shine upon us. And truly, when I invoke the power of Your name, Yahweh, upon my children, You bless them. So I ask You now to bless my children mightily. In Jesus' name I pray. Amen.

FOR FURTHER THOUGHT

- What was the result of the Jews' constantly blessing people in greeting?
- In what ways does God favor and prosper those we bless?
- What happens when you bless your children in the name of the Lord?
- What does this mean: "They will put my name on the Israelites" (Numbers 6:27)?

16.

PRAYER WHEN YOU'RE DISCOURAGED

As a mother, you find great fulfillment in knowing your children's needs are met and they are content. But one of the most disheartening things is for them—intentionally or unintentionally—to make you feel like a failure for not providing something they have their hearts set on.

One day when the Israelites were living in the Sinai desert, everyone in the camp began wailing, "Oh that someone would give us meat to eat! For we were well-off in Egypt." By "someone" they didn't mean God, and they made this plain by confronting Moses and insisting, "Give us meat that we may eat!" But where on earth could he get enough meat out in the desert to feed about two million people? And why couldn't they simply be content with the miraculous manna God had provided? The truth was, they had more than enough to eat already.

Their complaints caused Moses to become deeply discouraged. He prayed to God, "Why have You been so hard on Your servant? And why have I not found favor in Your sight, that You have laid the burden of all this people on me? Was it I who conceived all this people? Was it I who brought them forth, that You should say to me, 'Carry them in your bosom as a nurse carries a nursing infant, to the land which You swore to their fathers'?" (Numbers 11:11–12 NASB).

At some point in your life, you've probably identified with what Moses prayed here. Your children should be old enough to understand that they can't have everything they want, yet here they are, insisting on something. And here you are, feeling like a failure because you can't provide it. Moses continued praying: "Where am I to get meat to give to all this people? . . . I alone am not able to carry all this people, because it is too burdensome for me. So if You are going to deal thus with me, please kill me at once, if I have found favor in Your sight, and do not let me see my wretchedness" (vv. 13–15 NASB).

Sometimes what your children do and say affects you at a basic gut level. Moses felt like such a failure, so wretched and worthless, that he prayed to die. But God didn't take Moses' life. Instead he said, "Gather for Me seventy men from the elders of Israel. . .and they shall bear the burden of the people with you" (vv. 16–17 NASB).

Think of it: Moses felt like such a failure that he despaired of living. Have you ever felt that way? Thank God He doesn't answer when you pray in times of discouragement. Instead, He looks beyond your emotions, sees the problem, and sends a solution that matches your problem.

Sometimes your children may act this way. Instead of praying for God to supply something they long for and having the patience to wait until He does—or learning to be content without it—they complain. But you'll collapse under the burden if you try to "carry them in your bosom" by giving them everything they want.

More often than not, the solution is found in praying that your children will accept the apostle Paul's advice: "I have learned to be content whatever the circumstances. I know what it is to be in need, and I know what it is to have plenty. I have learned the secret of being content in any and every situation. . .whether living in plenty or in want" (Philippians 4:11–12 NIV).

*Father in heaven, there are times when I identify
with what Moses prayed. I've allowed my children
to place unreasonable burdens and expectations
upon me, and I've nearly burned out trying to fulfill
these nonessential demands. But I wasn't meant to
carry such burdens. You're our Provider, and if You
haven't provided something they want, they'll have to
learn to do without it. Help them to be grateful for
what they do have and to know what they can and
can't expect. In Jesus' name I pray. Amen.*

FOR FURTHER THOUGHT

- Have you ever prayed a despondent prayer like Moses did?

- How have your children burdened you unknowingly by their demands?

- Often, what is God's answer to your kids' unreasonable demands?

17.

DON'T LIMIT GOD

When the Israelites were wailing for meat, God said, "The LORD heard you when you cried, 'Oh, for some meat!' . . . Now the LORD will give you meat, and you will have to eat it. And it won't be for just a day or two, or for five or ten or even twenty. You will eat it for a whole month until you gag and are sick of it."

Moses, with his limited understanding, couldn't see how God could provide like *that*. He prayed, "There are 600,000 foot soldiers here with me, and yet you say, 'I will give them meat for a whole month!' Even if we butchered all our flocks and herds, would that satisfy them? Even if we caught all the fish in the sea, would that be enough?" Moses considered the only options he thought were available and frankly blurted out his doubt.

The Lord replied, "Has my arm lost its power? Now you will see whether or not my word comes true!"

Shortly thereafter, God sent a wind that swept in vast flocks of quail. Every March and April they migrate from Africa to Europe, and their route crosses the Sinai desert. So God brought *all* the migrating quail at once and wore them out with heavy winds. Exhausted birds dropped to the ground inside the camp and for miles in every direction. The Israelites went out and gathered literal tons of quail! (Numbers 11:18–23, 31–32 NLT).

Now, it wasn't a sin that Moses couldn't understand how God would do such a miracle, but where his attitude was wrong was in basically stating, "There are only two ways we could end up with a large quantity of meat, God. Either (a) we butcher all our flocks and herds, or (b) we catch all the fish in the sea. But neither option will last us a *month*." Yet all along, God was planning option (c): blow in migrating quail.

The smartest thing Moses could have done would have been to pray and ask God what He was going to do. That's what Mary did. When the angel Gabriel told her, "You will conceive in your womb and bring forth a Son," Mary was astonished, so she asked, "How can this be. . . ?" (Luke 1:31, 34 NKJV). So Gabriel explained. Satisfied, Mary believed. Moses also could have prayed, "How are You going to do this, Lord?"

So often, people put limits on God. The Bible says about the Israelites: "Again and again they tempted God, and limited the Holy One of Israel" (Psalm 78:41 NKJV). Sometimes people don't understand how God will solve a problem, so they end up thinking He *can't* solve it. They don't understand how there will be enough funds for their children's needs, so they conclude that God can't provide. But God is always bursting out of the narrow confines within which people seek to place Him.

The problem, however, is that when you come to the conclusion that God *can't* do a miracle, you don't bother to pray anymore. Then He definitely won't act.

Mothers do have an advantage over fathers here. God made men to be practical problem-solvers. By nature, they look at problems logically, analyze the available facts, and draw the most reasonable conclusions. This ability stands them in good stead most of the time, especially when they're dealing with mechanical problems and rational issues. But this approach has very real limitations and grinds to a shuddering halt when you introduce the supernatural. And God is supernatural.

Mothers are more intuitive by nature; they often draw conclusions from sources other than just rational reasons and facts. Plus they're more relational and interdependent, so they more naturally reach out for help—including reaching out to God.

Dear God, please forgive me for placing limitations on You, trying to box You in by telling You the narrow confines You must work within. Sometimes I tie Your hands, then get impatient and frustrated when You "don't answer prayer." Help me to truly get my mind around this one fact: You are far bigger and more resourceful than I am, and You aren't limited to the paltry solutions I can offer. Help me to widen my horizons and trust You. In Jesus' name I pray. Amen.

FOR FURTHER THOUGHT

- Why is men's rational problem-solving approach often very limited? How do women help balance that?

- When you think God can't do a miracle, how does this affect your prayers?

- How is God limited when you tell Him exactly how He must answer your prayer?

18.

PRAYING FOR THE YOUNG GENERATION

Moses sent twelve spies north into Canaan, and after forty days, they returned. Ten of them reported that they didn't stand a chance of defeating the Canaanites. The people were too strong and their cities were too fortified. Only Joshua and Caleb insisted that, with the Lord's help, they could conquer the land.

The ten spies so discouraged the Israelites that they cried, "Would that we had died in this wilderness! Why is the LORD bringing us into this land, to fall by the sword? Our wives and our little ones will become plunder" (Numbers 14:2–3 NASB). God was so angry over their failure to trust Him that He wanted to slay them all on the spot.

But Moses pleaded, "I pray, let the power of the Lord be great, just as You have declared, 'The LORD is slow to anger and abundant in lovingkindness, forgiving iniquity and transgression. . . .' Pardon, I pray, the iniquity of this people according to the greatness of Your lovingkindness, just as You also have forgiven this people, from Egypt even until now" (vv. 17–19 NASB). Moses reminded God that He had forgiven the Israelites many times already. Why destroy them now after having gone through so much with them and bringing them so far?

The Lord answered, "I have pardoned them. . .*but*. . ." (vv. 20–21 NASB). This was a big "but." None of the disbelieving older generation would enter the Promised Land. God wouldn't slay them this instant, but they *would* die of old age in the desert—only the younger generation would enter Canaan.

God declared to the older generation, "Just as you have spoken in My hearing, so I will surely do to you; your corpses will fall in this wilderness. . . . Your children, however, whom you said would become a prey—I will bring them in, and they will know the land which you have rejected. . . . Your sons shall be shepherds for forty years in the wilderness, and they will suffer for your unfaithfulness" (vv. 28–29, 31, 33 NASB). Some people think it's unfair that God would make the children suffer for their parents' sins, but He had a loving, redemptive purpose in His decision.

To the *younger* generation God declared:

> *"You shall remember all the way which the LORD your God has led you in the wilderness these forty years, that He might humble you, testing you, to know what was in your heart, whether you would keep His commandments or not. He humbled you and let you be hungry, and fed you with manna. . .that He might make you understand that man does not live by bread alone, but man lives by everything that proceeds out of the mouth of the LORD. . . . Thus you are to know in your heart that the LORD your God was disciplining you just as a man disciplines his son." (Deuteronomy 8:2–3, 5 NASB)*

Moses was focused on God forgiving and sparing the disobedient older generation, whereas God was focused on sparing and caring for their children.

At times God spares a disobedient people for the

sake of their innocent children (Jonah 4:10–11), but Moses never thought of this or gave it for a reason when he prayed. Moses never even thought to ask God to spare the children, even if He was determined to slay the older generation. Probably the only reason God spared them as long as He did was so they could care for their children.

Sometimes it never occurs to Christian parents to pray for their children. They think that as long as their children are happy, healthy, and attending Sunday school, they'll be okay. Besides, they have more "important," pressing things to pray about. So they overlook their children. But God has great plans for them. The Bible says of the righteous, "Their children will be mighty in the land" (Psalm 112:2 NIV). Your children need lots of prayer. Don't neglect to pray for them.

Dear God, help me, like You, to be focused on my children. Help me to train them in Your ways. Even days when I am exhausted, help me to give smiles, hugs, and encouraging words. In Jesus' name I pray. Amen.

FOR FURTHER THOUGHT

- Moses never thought to ask God to spare the children. Why might that have been?
- What was the difference between Moses' focus and God's focus?
- What is the difference between God's judgment and His loving discipline?

19.

Praying Through Behavioral Issues

If you have a naturally well-behaved, polite child, you may be tempted to have a smug attitude when watching other parents deal with a strong-willed, whining child. You may be tempted to think that you have superior parenting skills or that your child is much more mature. But be careful: your child might surprise you too.

This happened with the children of Israel. After the doubting, disobedient older generation had died, it was time for the believing, obedient younger generation to enter Canaan. But first they had to march south though the Arabah, around Edom. There is hardly a more desolate region on earth, and "the soul of the people became very discouraged on the way" (Numbers 21:4 NKJV).

It was stifling hot and bone-dry. There was no water or food. God, however, faithfully continued to send manna. But the people were hot and thirsty and asked Moses, "Why have you brought us up out of Egypt to die in the wilderness?" They bitterly complained, "There is no food and no water, and our soul loathes this worthless bread" (v. 5 NKJV). Manna was anything but worthless. It was packed with so much nutritional value that it alone sustained the daily needs of the Israelites.

This wasn't the older generation speaking. You would expect *them* to have doubted and murmured. They had done that from the beginning and had complained nearly every step of the way after leaving Egypt. But this was the younger generation bitterly complaining! Yes, they were burning up in the heat. True, there was no water. It *was* a real test of their faith, but it exposed who they were under pressure.

Until this time, there hadn't been one recorded complaint or doubt to mar their reputation. They were Moses' pride and joy, the "good" generation of Israelites who were destined to march in and conquer Canaan. And now they were accusing both Moses and God of failing them.

God was so angry that He sent serpents into their camp, which bit them. Soon they were dying. Realizing their sin, they hurried to Moses and confessed, "We have sinned, for we have spoken against the LORD and against you; pray to the LORD that He take away the serpents from us" (v. 7 NKJV). So Moses prayed for them. His prayer isn't recorded, but you can be sure that he asked God to forgive the people, to send the snakes away, and to heal those who'd been bitten.

Moses had no idea *how* God would heal the people. But the Lord instructed him, "Make a fiery serpent, and set it on a pole; and it shall be that everyone who is bitten, when he looks at it, shall live" (v. 8 NKJV). Moses probably had an Israelite metalworker grab the nearest bronze staff and hastily hammer it into the form of a serpent. Then they attached it to a pole, and everyone who had been bitten looked at it and lived.

It can be a real shock when a well-behaved child unexpectedly begins rebelling and talking back. Typically this happens—if it does happen—during a child's teen years. Suddenly you enter a whole new phase of your relationship. If you'd slacked off in your prayers for that child, this new phase gives you a good reason to focus on him or her in your daily prayers.

Solomon wrote, "Train up a child in the way he should go: and when he is old, he will not depart from it" (Proverbs 22:6 KJV). This biblical teaching is a general rule, however, not an unconditional promise. Many children from Christian homes have rebelled and departed from the training they received. Even children who don't depart permanently may go through a rebellious phase, especially when their lives are difficult or they're under pressure. It's up to you to pray for them during such times.

Lord, I thank You for the goodness of Your Word and Your Spirit and for the ability to invest in my children over the years. I trust I've laid a good foundation. I thank You for all the good things You have planned for their lives. Help them make it through these present behavioral issues and stay on track for the wonderful future you have for them. In Jesus' name I pray. Amen.

FOR FURTHER THOUGHT

- Why do even well-trained, "good" kids go through rebellious phases?
- What kind of adversity does it take to cause your children to complain?
- What does God expect you to do for your children during such times?

20.

ASKING GOD FOR PARENTAL WISDOM

In the days of the judges, "a certain man of Zorah, named Manoah. . .had a wife who was childless, unable to give birth. The angel of the LORD appeared to her and said, 'You are barren and childless, but you. . .will become pregnant and have a son whose head is never to be touched by a razor because the boy is to be a Nazirite, dedicated to God from the womb. He will take the lead in delivering Israel from the hands of the Philistines'" (Judges 13:2–3, 5 NIV). This child was Samson.

Manoah's wife hurried to him and told him that a man of God, as awesome in appearance as an angel, had spoken to her.

> *Then Manoah prayed to the LORD: "Pardon your servant, Lord. I beg you to let the man of God you sent to us come again to teach us how to bring up the boy who is to be born." God heard Manoah, and the angel of God came again. . . . So Manoah asked him, "When your words are fulfilled, what is to be the rule that governs the boy's life and work?" The angel of the LORD answered, "Your wife must do all that I have told her. She must not eat anything that comes from the grapevine, nor drink any wine or other fermented drink nor eat anything unclean. She must do everything I have commanded her." (vv. 8–10, 12–14 NIV)*

Manoah later realized that this was the Angel of the Lord, a manifestation of God Himself, and exclaimed, "We have seen God!" (vv. 21–22 NIV).

Manoah had prayed, "Teach us how to bring up the boy," and asked, "What is to be the rule that governs the boy's life and work?" These are two of the best prayers you can pray as a mother. They demonstrated Manoah's dependence on God. Proverbs 3:5–6 (NKJV) says, "Trust in the LORD with all your heart, and lean not on your own understanding; in all your ways acknowledge Him, and He shall direct your paths."

God has planted certain instincts within the heart of every parent. You naturally desire to protect, love, nurture, and instruct your children. Do these basic things, and you will normally achieve success.

Yet certain parenting skills will be beyond your normal abilities. After all, each child is a unique creation of God, so you need His supernatural wisdom in how best to relate to them, and you need Him to "direct your paths" so you can help your child fully blossom. And certainly, if one of your children has an outstanding gift and a unique calling, you'll need great insight into how best to raise them. Like Manoah, you gain such insight by asking the Lord for His help and guidance.

Parents of special-needs children also must go through a learning curve as they discover the special environmental requirements, dietary needs, and other factors involved in raising their child safely and well. Often parents find that meeting such needs requires a change in their *own* lifestyle and attitude. For example, the Lord's instructions for Samson's development involved special dietary restrictions that his mother was to follow while he was forming in her womb (Judges 13:14).

"The woman gave birth to a boy and named him Samson. He grew and the LORD blessed him, and the Spirit of the LORD began to stir him" (vv. 24–25 NIV). God Himself will supernaturally bless your children, and His Spirit will stir up His gifts within them, but your part as a parent is also vital to their success. You must *help* to stir up gifts nascent within your child. "I remind you to stir up the gift of God which is in you" (2 Timothy 1:6 NKJV). And if you pray, God will give you the wisdom you need to do exactly that.

Dear God, thank You for giving me such wonderful children. Each one has special talents and abilities, and You have a unique purpose for each of their lives, even if they don't seem to be especially outstanding or extraordinary. Help me to do my part to encourage and nurture each of my children. Give me wisdom to know how to stir up the gift of God within them and to inspire them to dedicate their lives and talents to You. In Jesus' name I pray. Amen.

FOR FURTHER THOUGHT

- What unique gifts does each of your children possess?
- Have you asked God to show you how to nurture your child's special talents?
- How do you and God work together to stir up your child's gifts?
- How do all these lessons apply to special-needs children?

21.

PRAYING FOR ADOPTED CHILDREN

A woman named Hannah was desperate for a child, so she prayed, "LORD Almighty, if you will only look on your servant's misery and remember me, and not forget your servant but give her a son, then I will give him to the LORD for all the days of his life." Later she happily said, "I prayed for this child, and the LORD has granted me what I asked of him" (1 Samuel 1:11, 27 NIV). But she never forgot her promise.

Because the adoption process can be very difficult at times and can put you and your husband through an emotional roller-coaster ride, you'll find yourselves praying more than you've ever prayed before. But the joy you feel when you finally bring home your new child makes all the struggles worth it. Your praying isn't done, but now you can pour love and joy into your prayers for your growing child.

Yes, you will experience challenging moments. Adopted children may seem perfect when you first bring them home, but like everyone else, they're sinners in need of salvation. Along with giving you great joy, they will disobey you, upset you, and try your patience. But don't ever lose sight of the original thankfulness you had for them.

In past decades it was common for parents not to tell adopted children that they weren't biological offspring. The parents either felt there was a stigma to being adopted or worried that such knowledge would affect the parent-child relationship negatively. Thankfully, these days people are more open about the subject, and adopted children are usually secure in their parents' love, realizing their parents deliberately chose them and *are* their parents in every other way that counts.

The Bible shines a spotlight on adoption, showing what a beautiful thing it can be. God definitely believes in it. He has adopted millions of people of all ages as His children. "He predestined us to adoption as sons through Jesus Christ to Himself, according to the kind intention of His will" (Ephesians 1:5 NASB; see also Romans 8:15; Galatians 4:5). He promises, "I will be a father to you, and you shall be sons and daughters to Me" (2 Corinthians 6:18 NASB). Your children belong to the Lord, and you can be very thankful for that.

Paul describes God's "kind intention" this way: we were like a branch cut off of a wild olive tree and spliced into a richly cultivated olive tree. "You Gentiles, who were branches from a wild olive tree, have been grafted in. So now you also receive the blessing. . .sharing in the rich nourishment from the root of God's special olive tree" (Romans 11:17 NLT).

On a related theme, Paul considered certain young men his sons and called them "children" and "sons." To a Christian named Philemon, he wrote about a runaway slave he had led to the Lord in Rome, "I appeal to you for my child Onesimus, whom I have begotten in my imprisonment" (Philemon 1:10 NASB). Paul called another young man, Timothy, "my beloved son" (2 Timothy 1:2 NASB). In another letter Paul said of him, "You know of his proven worth, that he served with me in the furtherance of the gospel like a child serving his father" (Philippians 2:22 NASB).

Parents sometimes say even of their natural children, "They're not really *my* children. They're just on loan from God." That's why, in fact, you dedicate your children to the Lord—give them back to Him. The same is true of adopted children. Although they'll always be your children, they belong to the Lord first and foremost. So always remember to pray that they'll look to God as their Father in heaven.

Father in heaven, thank You that in Your
great love You saw me when I was lost and alone,
adopted me as Your own child, and brought me into
Your family. For that I am eternally grateful. Thank
You also that my husband and I have been able to
adopt a child and raise him/her as our very own.
Help us to be good parents, and teach us how to raise
this child. Help him/her to be secure in our love and
to grow up to be the wonderful person You intend
him/her to be. In Jesus' name. Amen.

FOR FURTHER THOUGHT

- How is adopting a child similar to what God did by saving you?
- What are the special challenges of adopting that you need to pray about?
- How can being an adoptive parent be especially rewarding?

22.

RECOGNIZING GOD'S VOICE

The prophet Samuel was about twelve years old when he first heard God speak. It so happened one night, before the lamp of God went out in the tabernacle, that the old high priest Eli was lying down in his chamber and Samuel was lying in his room. Then the Lord called Samuel's name. He answered, "Here I am!" There was no answer, so he got up and ran to Eli. Entering his chamber, Samuel said, "Here I am, for you called me." But Eli answered, "I did not call; lie down again." Puzzled, Samuel walked back to his room and returned to bed.

Then the Lord called again, "Samuel!" Again Samuel arose, went to Eli, and said, "Here I am, for you called me." Eli answered, "I did not call, my son; lie down again."

Then the Lord called Samuel a third time. Again he arose, went to Eli, and said, "Here I am, for you did call me." Then Eli realized that God had called the boy. So Eli said to him, "Go, lie down; and it shall be, if He calls you, that you must say, 'Speak, LORD, for Your servant hears.'" So Samuel went and lay down again.

The Lord called a fourth time, "Samuel! Samuel!" So he answered, "Speak, for Your servant hears" (1 Samuel 3:4–10 NKJV). Then the Lord told Samuel that He would judge Eli and his sons for their sins. (Some years later, God followed through on this pronouncement and then used Samuel to lead the people back to God.)

This story shows how easy it can be to mistake God's voice for other voices. Many people today, however, instead of hearing *God's* voice and thinking a *person* is speaking, tune in to the jumbled thoughts of their own mind and think they're hearing from God. Consequently, they're disappointed when what they've heard in their mind doesn't happen or doesn't work out.

Now, you should teach your children that God *does* still speak today, but it's important to establish that the primary way He speaks is through His written Word, the Bible. That's why they need to read the Bible faithfully and think about what it means. Then when God wants to speak to them, He can lead them to read scriptures they're already familiar with. For example, if they've had a fight with someone and pray for God's perspective, He may well lead them to reread 1 Corinthians 13. They already know it's the Love Chapter, but God wants them to be reminded of certain clear, powerful thoughts in it that they've forgotten.

In addition, Jesus promised, "The Holy Spirit. . .will teach you everything and will remind you of everything I have told you" (John 14:26 NLT). Often God's Spirit will bring a specific Bible passage to your child's mind. It will be a verse or a portion of a verse they've read previously, and God speaks to them by highlighting it in their memory.

And though God *can* still speak audibly like He did to Samuel, usually when He chooses to give specific direction or guidance, He communicates in a "still small voice" (1 Kings 19:12 KJV). Your child may hear specific words, but often they will simply have a strong impression that they should or shouldn't do something, go somewhere, or say something. In other words, God speaks to their conscience.

How can children know whether thoughts are of God, of their own busy mind, or of the enemy? One of the easiest ways to know the difference is if the thought is telling them to do something selfish or unselfish, spiteful or kind. God will send good, positive, loving thoughts into their mind, because "God's love has been poured out into our hearts through the Holy Spirit, who has been given to us" (Romans 5:5 NIV).

Like Samuel, your children must learn to hear and obey the voice of God if they are to walk in God's will for their lives.

Father, please help my children to truly hear Your voice and to be guided by You in all their decisions. Give them a great love for Your Word, and help them to be faithful in their daily Bible reading. Please help them to understand what they read, and most importantly, give them determination to obey it. Help them not to be stubborn, to insist on their own will, or to mistake their own thoughts for Your voice. In Jesus' name. Amen.

FOR FURTHER THOUGHT

- When God desires to speak to His children, how does He normally do it?

- Why is it so easy to mistake your own thoughts for God's voice?

- What is one of the easiest ways to tell whether a thought is from God?

23.

A Father in Israel

Deborah was a "mother in Israel" (Judges 5:7 KJV), and Elisha was a father in Israel. When Elisha was dying, the king of Israel wept, "O my father, my father" (2 Kings 13:14 NKJV). Spiritual fathers were the larger-than-life men who arose, anointed by God, to lead the people. Like Elisha after him, the prophet Samuel was also a father in Israel.

Samuel was a spiritual leader. He led Israel in a revival and anointed two kings. Samuel was a prophet as well. He spoke the word of the Lord accurately and boldly and even rebuked and corrected King Saul. Samuel was a military leader. He led the armies of Israel in victorious battles. And finally, Samuel was a great intercessor who prayed constantly for his people. He said, "As for me, far be it from me that I should sin against the LORD by failing to pray for you. And I will teach you the way that is good and right" (1 Samuel 12:23 NIV).

Samuel was considered the greatest man of God since Moses (Jeremiah 15:1). But even he didn't have a perfect track record. Despite his godly example and many prayers, his own sons went astray—though he surely must have poured out his heart to God for them.

"It came about when Samuel was old that he appointed his sons judges over Israel. . . . His sons, however, did not walk in his ways, but turned aside after dishonest gain and took bribes and perverted justice. Then all the elders of Israel. . .said to him, 'Behold, you have grown old, and your sons do not walk in your ways. Now appoint a king for us to judge us like all the nations.' But the thing was displeasing in the sight of Samuel" and he did what came naturally to him: "Samuel prayed to the LORD" (1 Samuel 8:1, 3–6 NASB).

Like Samuel, you may know the disappointment of having children who don't follow the Lord. If you haven't invested much time in training them and have "sinned against the Lord by failing to pray for them," then you bear much of the responsibility. But if you've done your best to raise them in the ways of the Lord (as Samuel surely did), then they alone are responsible for their disobedience. Samuel said, "Far be it from me that I should sin against the LORD by failing to pray for you. And I will teach you the way that is good and right." If he was doing these things for all Israel, he must have done them for his own sons. But they failed to respond.

Some Christians like to announce, "All *my* children are serving the Lord," and then take it upon themselves to blame others if any of their children go astray, insinuating that they must have failed as parents. But the Bible clearly teaches that righteous parents' children sometimes choose a sinful life, and wicked parents' children sometimes choose a righteous life (Ezekiel 18:5–18).

Unbelievers often especially enjoy accusing preachers, pointing out that a number of "preacher's kids" abandon the faith and seek a worldly life. These critics happily conclude that the preachers must have been hypocrites, or they neglected their children, or the whole concept of serving God must be a mistake since their children rejected it. This is simply not the case. Such people would have accused Samuel as well.

Jesus pointed out that the religious leaders criticized the lifestyles of both Him and John the Baptist, but in truth they were jealous of their popular appeal and results. As Jesus pointed out, "Wisdom is vindicated by all her children" (Luke 7:35 NASB). You might not always be vindicated by all your *natural* children—some of them might go astray for a while—but the wisdom of God *will* be vindicated by its results.

Dear God, You know I've done my best to follow You and to teach my children to do the same. Yet somehow they've gone astray. Lord, I commit them into Your hands and pray that You'll yet have mercy on them and bring them back to You. Lord, help me to continue walking faithfully before You and not to sin by neglecting to pray for my children. In Jesus' name I pray. Amen.

FOR FURTHER THOUGHT

- Is it always the parents' fault when their kids don't follow the Lord?
- Why do preachers so often get blamed for their children's moral failure?

24.

A SENSE OF AWE IN PRAYER

Children react with wonder and delight when gazing upward at the night sky crowded full of stars, seeing a lonely meteor slide down the heavens, or exploring the craters of the moon through a telescope. And these experiences cause older children to ask profound spiritual questions. When learning how vast the universe is and how small and insignificant they are by comparison, they're moved to ponder the immense power of God and their specific purpose in the big world around them.

David was overcome with a similar sense of awe when he wrote this prayer: "O LORD, our Lord, your majestic name fills the earth! Your glory is higher than the heavens. . . . When I look at the night sky and see the work of your fingers—the moon and the stars you set in place—what are mere mortals that you should think about them, human beings that you should care for them?" (Psalm 8:1, 3–4 NLT).

Another psalm declares, "He counts the number of the stars; He calls them all by name" (Psalm 147:4 NKJV). They're not just distant orbs of gas, unseen and unknown, lost in the depths of space with drab designations like HD 189276 or PSR B2016+28. God has a personal name for each one of them. Yet this same great God who created all the trillions upon quintillions of stars, and knows each of them personally, also knows and thinks about every single person on earth. Tell *that* to your child!

David's prayer above captures the sense of wonder

children experience when viewing creation in all its splendor. And when they see nature, they're getting a good idea of the Lord Himself. "God's invisible qualities—his eternal power and divine nature—have been clearly seen, being understood from what has been made" (Romans 1:20 NIV). David wrote elsewhere, "The heavens declare the glory of God; the skies proclaim the work of his hands" (Psalm 19:1 NIV).

It's fine for small children to repeat the same basic prayer night after night, and even memorized prayers have their place, but when they've contemplated creation in breathless awe, they're open to truly worship and know God. That's why it's helpful for you to introduce your child to nature. This may include visiting the zoo, camping in the great outdoors, gathering shells in the surf, strolling through a park, beholding a rainbow, gazing at the stars, gardening, and even watching nature shows. All of these create gateways for you to teach your child meaningful worship and prayer.

If you live out in the country surrounded by fields, woods, and deer and other wild animals—if you and your kids are treated to spectacular sunsets and you can lie on top of a haystack looking up at the stars—your job is so much easier. But if you live in the city or the suburbs, you'll need to pray for opportunities and be a little more intentional and creative.

Another way your child can experience awe of God is by considering the many miracles He does in the world today. Habakkuk wrote, "I have heard all about you, LORD. I am filled with awe by your amazing works" (Habakkuk 3:2 NLT). And in Psalm 66 we read, "Come and see the works of God; He is awesome in His doing toward the sons of men" (v. 5 NKJV).

God does many miracles, both large and small, that demonstrate His power and remind you He's still active in the world. He often shows up just when you need Him to and proves His love and care. "He comes in golden splendor; God comes in awesome majesty. The Almighty is beyond our reach and exalted in power" (Job 37:22–23 NIV). He is truly awesome!

Dear Father in heaven, I thank You for the beauties and marvels of Your creation and how they stir up a sense of wonder in my children's hearts. I pray that You would use these awe-filled moments to help them appreciate Your greatness and power and wisdom. Don't let prayer time be simply a boring ritual that we go through. Lead them to worship You and pray to You with a heart overflowing with delight and amazement. In Jesus' name I pray. Amen.

FOR FURTHER THOUGHT

- Which aspect of nature creates a sense of wonder in you personally?

- Why must children not only pray words but also worship God with their spirit?

- What can you do this week to help your child be more in awe of God?

25.

PRAYER IN THE CAVE OF ADULLAM

There will be times in your children's lives when they'll feel boxed in by constricting circumstances. Perhaps a sickness keeps them in bed for several days in a row; perhaps an injury prevents them from joining fun activities, so they must sit on the sidelines while others play; perhaps they're stymied by their inability to master a new skill; or maybe you've had to ground them for misbehavior.

They may think God has grounded them, and while you might wish you could do something to alleviate the situation, you may be unable to help. What has to be has to be. So the best you can do is pray that they'll learn patience and keep a positive attitude.

The title of Psalm 142 (NIV) reads: "A maskil of David. When he was in the cave. A prayer." This makes it one of his earliest psalms, written when he was hiding in the Cave of Adullam (1 Samuel 22:1), near the ancient city of the same name. This short psalm is an intense, emotional prayer to God. David wrote:

> *I cry aloud to the LORD; I lift up my voice to the
> LORD for mercy. I pour out before him my com-
> plaint; before him I tell my trouble. When my spirit
> grows faint within me, it is you who watch over my
> way. In the path where I walk people have hidden
> a snare for me. Look and see, there is no one at my
> right hand; no one is concerned for me. I have no
> refuge; no one cares for my life. I cry to you, LORD;*

I say, "You are my refuge, my portion in the land of the living." Listen to my cry, for I am in desperate need; rescue me from those who pursue me, for they are too strong for me. Set me free from my prison, that I may praise your name. (Psalm 142:1–7 NIV)

David probably moved to the cave when the rainy season began, when life out in the open had become miserable. For the next few months, he and his men hunkered down in the damp cavern. In Israel it often rains heavily for three days nonstop. You might think living in a cave would be fun, but David complained that it was like a prison (v. 7). And he couldn't leave. He was being hunted and was in real danger.

David had been a beloved, highly praised hero in Israel. Now he'd been vilified, and King Saul and his army were seeking to kill him. He'd been forced to flee his home, leaving his wife behind. It was in this context that he prayed to God, "You are my refuge, my portion in the land of the living." God was about all David had left. So he looked to Him for help.

Children often have very little patience and become bored quickly. They moan, "No one cares how bored I am," just after you've finished listening to them. It can be vexing to hear their complaints when there's little you can do, and when what they're going through is trivial compared to what you and others are facing.

Besides praying for your kids, you may need to pray for yourself, that you'll have patience and not lose your temper. Yes, your children should respect your authority and learn to put up with a little boredom uncomplainingly, but be aware that they're already stressed and don't ride roughshod over their feelings with demands that they be quiet. The Bible says, "Fathers, do not exasperate your children, so that they will not lose heart" (Colossians 3:21 NASB).

This trial will soon be past and they'll be free to join in group activities again. Until then, you may need to pray and bite your tongue. . .at the same time.

Father, I pray that my children will have patience and an uncomplaining spirit when forced to sit out on fun activities. But because they are only kids— meaning I'll probably have to listen to a fair amount of grumbling—I pray that You'll give me patience and a slow temper. Help them to respect my authority, and help me to demonstrate wisdom and understanding. Father, help us all to get through this difficult time. In Jesus' name I pray. Amen.

FOR FURTHER THOUGHT

- What kinds of circumstances make your children feel like they're in prison?
- What do you pray when your kids are down about being sidelined or excluded?
- Why might you need to pray for yourself when your kids are bored?

26.

GUIDANCE IN TROUBLED TIMES

One of the most painful experiences a child can suffer is to be ostracized, whether at school or in the local neighborhood. Some leader of the pack gets the idea that your child isn't cool, doesn't wear the right clothing, or has some minor defect and then begins picking on her. Then the rest of the clique turns on your child. They either simply exclude her or go out of their way to try to make her life miserable. At times like this, you need to uphold her in prayer.

David knew what being ostracized was like. When King Saul turned against him and was pursuing him, many Israelites—believing David was now an "enemy"—became convinced it was their patriotic duty to betray him. As a result, David constantly fled through the wilderness, unsure of where to turn or whom to trust. One wrong step, one false friend, could spell his doom. He exclaimed, "There is but a step between me and death" (1 Samuel 20:3 NKJV). So he prayed:

> *Hear my prayer, O LORD, give ear to my supplications! . . . For the enemy has persecuted my soul. . . . Therefore my spirit is overwhelmed within me; my heart within me is distressed. . . . Answer me speedily, O LORD; my spirit fails! Do not hide Your face from me, lest I be like those who go down into the pit. Cause me to hear Your lovingkindness in the morning, for in You do I trust; cause me to know the way in which I should walk, for I lift*

up my soul to You. Deliver me, O LORD, from my
enemies; in You I take shelter. Teach me to do Your
will, for You are my God; Your Spirit is good.
Lead me in the land of uprightness.
(Psalm 143:1, 3–4, 7–10 NKJV)

Maybe your child's issue, however, isn't being ostracized and unsure of whom to trust. Perhaps he is simply wandering through a challenging season without direction, like in a wilderness, not knowing which way to turn or what choices to make. This is especially true of teens who must begin selecting a career path in high school. One choice may lead to success and another to a life of hardship. . .but at the onset both paths may seem equal. During such stressful times, be diligent to uphold your child in prayer.

David prayed, "My spirit is overwhelmed. . . . Cause me to hear Your lovingkindness." When your daughter is drifting and feeling discouraged day after day, the reminder that God loves her and is with her can make her whole week. You can pray this verse over her: "Send me a sign of your favor. . . . For you, O LORD, help and comfort me" (Psalm 86:17 NLT). Likewise, letting your son know that you're praying for him to receive clear direction will encourage him.

"Teach me to do Your will, for You are my God." It's important for your child to learn how to make wise career decisions, but even more importantly, he needs to choose to live by godly principles. If the Lord is his God, he will seek His will and God will show him. As a parent, you should pray that your child develops this kind of deep personal relationship with the Lord.

"Cause me to know the way in which I should walk." When her spiritual life is on the right foundation, your daughter can confidently ask God to lead her in practical matters. He has promised: "Commit your way to the LORD, trust also in Him, and He shall bring it to pass" (Psalm 37:5 NKJV). Always be faithful to pray that the Lord will help your children look to Him for guidance.

Dear God, I pray for my child who's being ostracized by the popular kids. Help her to know who her true friends are and to be satisfied with them. Help her to know that You are the Friend who will never forsake her. I also pray for my child who's feeling lost and overwhelmed, uncertain which way to turn. Help him to seek Your face and to make wise, godly decisions. In Jesus' name I pray. Amen.

FOR FURTHER THOUGHT

- What should you pray for your child when he/she is shunned or excluded?
- How can even a small sign of God's favor greatly encourage your child?
- What kind of relationship with God do you hope your child develops? How can you pray for this?

27.

ENCOURAGED TO PRAY

David and his men had left their wives and children in Ziklag—safe, so they thought—but in their absence, Amalekite raiders from the southern deserts attacked, burned the town, and took everything. When David's men returned to Ziklag, they were stunned.

"David and his men came to the city, and there it was, burned with fire; and their wives, their sons, and their daughters had been taken captive. Then David and the people who were with him lifted up their voices and wept, until they had no more power to weep. . . . Now David was greatly distressed, for the people spoke of stoning him, because the soul of all the people was grieved, every man for his sons and his daughters." But instead of giving up and going under, "David strengthened himself in the LORD his God."

David asked the Lord, "Shall I pursue this troop? Shall I overtake them?"

God answered, "Pursue, for you shall surely overtake them and without fail recover all" (1 Samuel 30:3–4, 6, 8 NKJV).

So David and his men began tracking the raiders. Along the way, they found a half-dead Egyptian, and David learned that he'd been a slave of the Amalekites but his master had abandoned him when he became sick. David asked him, "Can you take me down to this troop?" (v. 15 NKJV). The Egyptian agreed and led them to the Amalekite camp, and there they were, spread out and off guard, eating and drinking and dancing, rejoicing over all the spoil they had taken.

David's men attacked them from twilight until the evening of the next day. They fought fiercely, utterly routed the Amalekites, and recovered all that they had carried away. "Nothing of theirs was lacking, either small or great, sons or daughters, spoil or anything which they had taken from them; David recovered all" (v. 19 NKJV). What a powerful answer to prayer!

Sometimes you'll suffer a disaster and feel overwhelmed. Perhaps you sinned and failed God, and now the devil is trying to convince you that God is obliged to shut out your prayer and punish you—so you should just call it quits and not bother praying. This is one of his most clever lies. Instead, do like David did: "David strengthened himself in the LORD," reminding himself that God loved him—and not only that, but that God could do the impossible in desperate situations. Once he was assured of that truth, David was encouraged to pray and believe for a miracle.

Sometimes it will seem that your sons and daughters have been taken captive by the enemy. Perhaps they've backslidden from the Lord and been caught up in a worldly lifestyle. You need to pray for them, that "God perhaps will grant them repentance, so that they may know the truth, and that they may come to their senses and escape the snare of the devil, having been taken captive by him to do his will" (2 Timothy 2:25–26 NKJV).

Refuse to give up, refuse to stop trusting the Lord, and turn to God in prayer. You may feel the situation is hopeless, but during similarly dark times, Nehemiah admonished the Jews, "Remember the Lord, great and awesome, and fight for your brethren, your sons, your daughters, your wives, and your houses" (Nehemiah 4:14 NKJV).

But know this: it may not be a quick and easy battle, so to steel your resolve, you first must "strengthen yourself in the LORD." You do this by reading His Word and praying passionately. King Asa prayed, "LORD, there is no one besides You to help in the battle between the powerful and those who have no strength; so help us, O LORD our God, for we trust in You" (2 Chronicles 14:11 NASB). And Psalm 68:35 (NASB) tells us, "The God of Israel Himself gives strength and power to the people." Similarly, we read in Isaiah 40:31 (NKJV) that "those who wait on the LORD shall renew their strength."

God, thank You for this inspiring story about fighting discouragement and going on to gain a great victory, rescuing sons and daughters. Help me to have the same faith and resolve as David and his men had, and as Nehemiah and his men had. Help me to contend for my children, to lift them up in prayer and intercede for them wholeheartedly. In Jesus' name I pray. Amen.

FOR FURTHER THOUGHT

- Have your sons or daughters been taken captive by some enemy?
- Do you feel ready to give up? What should you do instead?
- What exactly can you do to encourage yourself in the Lord?
- Has God ever delivered your children from any form of captivity?

28.

STEADY THROUGH THE STORM

Sometimes things will go along so smoothly and peacefully that you'll feel like God's pet. But other times your family may be in an uproar, with one or more of your children experiencing severe testing—especially when they're going through puberty and their hormones seem intent on causing a train wreck. They appear to be lurching from one crisis to another. Barely do they survive one test when another comes along. You may wonder what's happening.

Many people in the Bible also experienced an unrelenting series of tests. After he defeated the Amalekites, with Saul dead, David went to Hebron where he was crowned king of Judah. Then he immediately became embroiled in a seven-year civil war with the northern tribes. No sooner was David proclaimed king of all Israel than the Philistines invaded. David defeated them but then was forced to battle several other nations, one after another. Despite many troubles and some near defeats, David gained great victories.

Second Samuel 22 begins by declaring, "David sang this song to the Lord on the day the Lord rescued him from all his enemies and from Saul. He sang: 'The Lord is my rock, my fortress, and my savior; my God is my rock, in whom I find protection. He is my shield, the power that saves me, and my place of safety. . . . I called on the Lord, who is worthy of praise, and he saved me from my enemies' " (2 Samuel 22:1–4 NLT).

David prayed, "O Lord, you are my lamp. The Lord

lights up my darkness. . . . You have given me your shield of victory; your help has made me great. You have made a wide path for my feet to keep them from slipping. . . . For this, O LORD, I will praise you among the nations; I will sing praises to your name. You give great victories to your king; you show unfailing love to your anointed" (vv. 29, 36–37, 50–51 NLT).

You may wonder if David's song possibly applies to your children's lives. They may feel defeated, frustrated, and desperate for a breakthrough. Their feet may be slipping. You may not feel that God has made them great. You may not feel that He's showing them unfailing love. But remember, David was frequently on the verge of defeat (vv. 5–7, 18–19). Then he would pray, and God would bring victory again and again. So, yes, your children can identify with this prayer.

Paul wrote, "Now thanks be to God who *always* leads us in triumph in Christ" (2 Corinthians 2:14 NKJV, emphasis added). It may not seem like your children are always triumphing, but God brings many victories out of what seem like defeats. And He keeps your children back from the brink of total defeat. As one psalm puts it, "The LORD has chastened me severely, but He has not given me over to death" (Psalm 118:18 NKJV).

During times like these, you may end up praying quite a bit more than you care to. If you were slacking off on prayer time before, you're definitely all caught up now. But don't grow weary. You need a stable, firm hand on the rudder during the height of the storm if you're to guide your ship safely to port. Your children may not appreciate what you're doing now, but they will when they get a bit of distance and perspective. So keep on praying!

God needs praying parents to keep their children on track during just such difficult times, so be sure to answer His call when He puts a burden on your heart to pray.

Lord, You've allowed my family to go through intense tests. At different points, at least from my perspective, my children's lives have been in chaos. They're on a roller-coaster ride, up one moment and down the next. Lord, send peace into their lives. Help them through these emotional crises. Help their hormones to stabilize. I trust that You'll see us through these storms and bring us into a peaceful haven. In Jesus' name I pray. Amen.

FOR FURTHER THOUGHT

- David sang an upbeat song, but did he experience victory all the time?

- Why would many people have given up if they'd been in David's shoes?

- Why are near disasters and defeats not necessarily the end?

29.

GOD, FULFILL YOUR PROMISES

One day David informed the prophet Nathan that he desired to build a house for the Lord. By this he meant a temple where God's Spirit could reside and where His people could worship Him. The next day, Nathan told David one of his descendants would build God a house, but God would build *David's* house.

Nathan prophesied, "The LORD also declares to you that the LORD will make a house for you. . . . Your house and your kingdom shall endure before Me forever; your throne shall be established forever" (2 Samuel 7:11, 16 NASB).

Deeply moved, David prayed:

> *"O LORD God, the word that You have spoken concerning Your servant and his house, confirm it forever, and do as You have spoken. . . . May the house of Your servant David be established before You. . . . Your words are truth, and You have promised this good thing to Your servant. Now therefore, may it please You to bless the house of Your servant, that it may continue forever before You. For You, O Lord GOD, have spoken; and with Your blessing may the house of Your servant be blessed forever."* (vv. 25–26, 28–29 NASB)

Although David's sons only ruled Judah for another 410 years, God saw to it that his throne and kingdom would endure to all ages in David's descendant Jesus the Messiah (Psalm 89:3–4; Luke 1:32).

Notice that David repeated his request four times. Some people think he needn't have bothered asking God to make good on His promise. Why pray, "Do as You have spoken"? But the Bible says, "We are labourers together with God" (1 Corinthians 3:9 KJV). God wants us to pray and remind Him to fulfill His promises.

David knew that God had told Saul, "You have not kept the commandment of the LORD your God. . . . The LORD would have established your kingdom over Israel forever. But now your kingdom shall not continue" (1 Samuel 13:13–14 NKJV). David knew he could still lose the promise through disobedience, negligence, or lack of prayer, and he didn't want to take that chance.

Yes, God is all-powerful. And He wills that certain, specific things happen. Yet what He wills doesn't always automatically happen. Although God can do anything, He often limits Himself to acting in response to our prayers. Yes, even for things that are explicitly His will.

If you read the Bible, you see that God has a general, overall will for children: He wants them to have a father and a mother in a stable, loving home; He wants parents to protect children and generate the finances to provide their needs; He wants them to be happy and healthy; He wants them to do well in school and succeed in life; He wants them to follow Him faithfully.

But none of these things happen of their own accord. Not only do you as a parent need to work hard to bring them to pass, but you need to pray that God blesses your efforts and your children. Many times the people voted "most likely to succeed" *don't*, in fact, succeed. Their lives go off the rails, or for some reason they never arrive at the finish line and end up falling far short of their potential. Why is that?

There may be in your children a seed of greatness, but that potential can fail if the seed isn't properly watered and nurtured. And everything ultimately depends on God. Paul said, "I planted the seed, Apollos watered it, but God has been making it grow. So neither the one who plants nor the one who waters is anything, but only God, who makes things grow" (1 Corinthians 3:6–7 NIV). Often God only makes things grow if you *pray* and ask Him to.

Father, forgive me for sometimes having a lackadaisical attitude toward raising my children. I don't always want to discipline. But I know this is part of my responsibility as a mother. Forgive me also for being negligent in prayer for my children. I could give a dozen excuses, but in the end I know that if I'm concerned, I'll pray. So please give me the will, the patience, and the energy to be there for them. In Jesus' name. Amen.

FOR FURTHER THOUGHT

- Why do you need to pray that God will do what He promised to do?
- How are mothers "laborers together with God"? What exactly is *your* part?
- Does God have a specific will for *your* children's lives?

30.

REPENTING AND RECEIVING FORGIVENESS

One evening David was up on the flat roof of his palace when he happened to look down into a courtyard and see a beautiful woman named Bathsheba bathing. Her husband, Uriah, was away at war, so David had her brought to the palace and committed adultery with her. When she became pregnant, David summoned Uriah and tried to get him to sleep with her so he'd think the child was his. That effort failed, so David had Uriah killed (2 Samuel 11:1–17). When a prophet confronted David about these sins, David was overcome with remorse and repented. He prayed:

> *Have mercy upon me, O God, according to Your lovingkindness; according to the multitude of Your tender mercies, blot out my transgressions. Wash me thoroughly from my iniquity, and cleanse me from my sin. For I acknowledge my transgressions, and my sin is always before me. . . . Behold, I was brought forth in iniquity, and in sin my mother conceived me. . . . Wash me, and I shall be whiter than snow. . . . Hide Your face from my sins, and blot out all my iniquities. Create in me a clean heart, O God, and renew a steadfast spirit within me. Do not cast me away from Your presence, and do not take Your Holy Spirit from me. Restore to me the joy of Your salvation, and uphold me by Your generous Spirit. . . . The sacrifices of God*

are a broken spirit, a broken and a contrite
heart—these, O God, You will not despise.
(Psalm 51:1–3, 5, 7, 9–12, 17 NKJV)

The Law of Moses said that adulterers and murderers should die, but God heard David's heartfelt prayer and had mercy on him. Nevertheless, serious damage had been done and there were consequences, some of which lasted for years (2 Samuel 12:10–11; 13–14).

While children don't sin like that, they still may hurt others. A child might injure someone, start a fire, tell a lie that gets a friend in trouble, start a rumor that destroys a friendship, and so on. Now, some of the above aren't always sins—just mistakes—even if, to the injured party, there's little difference. The child who caused the problem may not always be able to tell the difference either.

As a parent, you must explain to your child what they did wrong, and once they've repented, you need to lead them in praying to God for forgiveness. They may not know exactly what to say. It's a beautiful thing to lead your child into the presence of their heavenly Father, teach them how to communicate honestly with Him, and impress upon them that He's willing to forgive. During the course of their life, they'll make many mistakes and sin against God and others. Learning as a child to repent and receive God's forgiveness will benefit them hugely later in life.

God promises, "Though your sins are like scarlet, they shall be as white as snow; though they are red like crimson, they shall be as wool" (Isaiah 1:18 NKJV). If your child is suffering from unrelenting regret, he or she can know God's forgiveness today. If the problem began between you and your child, make sure they *know* that you love them and have forgiven them. Paul advised, "You ought to forgive and comfort him, so that he will not be overwhelmed by excessive sorrow" (2 Corinthians 2:7 NIV).

It's good for children to have tender consciences, but once they repent, they must forgive themselves—just as God does. Be sure to pray for your child if they feel excessive guilt and talking about it doesn't completely resolve it. Pray that they may experience complete forgiveness and freedom from guilt. Your prayers will also have another effect: they will transform your *own* spirit, making your love and acceptance contagious—and this will go a long way toward helping your child recover.

Dear God, I thank You that You're merciful and forgiving and that You always forgive our sins when we come to You. If you forgave King David, You'll surely forgive me and my children. Help me to model Your forgiveness. Help me never to hold grudges against my children or refuse to pardon them. Loose them from the weight of past mistakes and sins, and help them to walk in freedom, fully forgiven. In Jesus' name. Amen.

FOR FURTHER THOUGHT

- Why do many children struggle to differentiate between mistakes and sins?

- What kinds of problems might arise when children can't forgive themselves?

- Do your children know that you always forgive them?

- Do your children know how to pray a prayer of repentance and find forgiveness?

31.

Now I Lay Me Down to Sleep

A "frenemy" is a so-called friend who is actually an enemy, and some women feel they have no choice but to maintain good relations with such people. As the king of Israel, David often had to entertain enemies who masqueraded as friends. He observed, "When one of them comes to see me, he speaks falsely, while his heart gathers slander; then he goes out and spreads it around" (Psalm 41:6 NIV).

David's worst frenemy was his son Absalom. This handsome, sweet-talking royal wanted to be king, so he organized a conspiracy and won many Israelites to his side. Then he marched on Jerusalem. But David was warned, fled the city, and marshaled his troops. Absalom's army followed, and the two armies clashed. Despite David's order not to harm Absalom, Joab executed him then sounded a trumpet. The battle was over. God had once again protected David (2 Samuel 15:10–13; 17:24–26; 18:1–17).

David wrote a short psalm just before the battle, proclaiming that he trusted God to protect him and he wouldn't fear. The title of Psalm 3 (NIV) reads, "A psalm of David. When he fled from his son Absalom." In this psalm, David prayed:

> LORD, how many are my foes! How many rise up
> against me! Many are saying of me, 'God will not
> deliver him.' But you, LORD, are a shield around
> me, my glory, the One who lifts my head high. I
> call out to the LORD, and he answers me from his

holy mountain. I lie down and sleep; I wake again,
because the LORD sustains me. I will not fear though
tens of thousands assail me on every side. Arise,
LORD! Deliver me, my God! (Psalm 3:1–7 NIV)

In the midst of David's battle prayer, he declared, "I lie down and sleep; I wake again, because the LORD sustains me." Though preparing for the greatest struggle of his life, he was able to lie down and sleep peacefully, without tossing and turning and worrying all night. Knowing that God was a shield around him and wouldn't allow him to be harmed even though multitudes assailed him, David refused to give in to fear.

When your children are little, you normally tuck them in and either pray for them or lead them in saying their prayers—or both. They learn to ask God to place His angels around them to protect them and to ask Him to give them sweet dreams. Children are sometimes afraid of the dark or frightened by nightmares and need to be assured that God is with them. A good promise to claim is Proverbs 3:24 (NIV): "When you lie down, you will not be afraid; when you lie down, your sleep will be sweet."

It's very important that you teach your children not only what to pray for but also how to quote promises from the Bible when they make their requests. Only God's Word can give them the authority to claim that God will take action for them. And if they have particular issues with fear of the dark or bad dreams, they should memorize and quote promises that counter these.

Knowing that God's angels guard them, your children can pray, "In peace I will lie down and sleep, for you alone, LORD, make me dwell in safety" (Psalm 4:8 NIV). Because of God's protection, they "will not fear the terror of night"

(Psalm 91:5 NIV). When they feel worried and have trouble sleeping, they can be assured that God "grants sleep to those he loves" (Psalm 127:2 NIV).

As your children grow older, they might not want you to pray with them as much as you used to, but you can still pray *for* them even if you're not in the same room.

Dear Father in heaven, I pray that You would be with my children when they sleep tonight. Help them to cast all the cares of their day upon You and to commit their problems and worries to You. Keep them from giving in to fear, and help them to trust in the promises of Your Word so their minds can be at peace. And give them sweet dreams, Lord. Drive back the enemy and put Your holy angels around my children to protect them. In Jesus' name. Amen.

FOR FURTHER THOUGHT

- How can praying for your children help them when they're afraid at night?
- How does quoting Bible promises benefit your children when they pray?
- Why is it important to pray that your children have peaceful dreams?

32.

Lord, Don't Be Silent

Any parent who has ever prayed repeatedly for a child's desperate need knows how frustrating it can be to face deafening silence when there's no answer. You may be left wondering if God has heard or if He even cares. God's "silence" doesn't necessarily refer to His refusal to speak words of encouragement. Often people think of God as being silent when He doesn't answer their prayers or do miracles in the way they hope.

A related image comes to mind—that of God hiding Himself when you need His help. David prayed, "Why do You stand afar off, O Lord? Why do You hide in times of trouble?" (Psalm 10:1 NKJV). Another time David prayed, "Do not hide Your face from me. . .do not leave me nor forsake me, O God of my salvation" (Psalm 27:9 NKJV).

This feeling of God being silent or abandoning you is something all believers experience at one time or another. It's difficult enough for you as an adult, but it's *much* harder for your children. King David often enjoyed times of communion with God, yet he also experienced times when God was inexplicably silent. David then poured out his heart, candidly asking God why He wasn't answering.

For example, when David was sick—so sick he felt like he was dying—he prayed: "Remove Your plague from me; because of the opposition of Your hand I am perishing. With reproofs You chasten a man for iniquity. . . . Hear my prayer, O Lord, and give ear to my cry; do not be silent at my tears" (Psalm 39:10–12 NASB). You can surely identify with this prayer if your children have ever been sick for a prolonged period.

Another time, David experienced God's silence despite many prayers when he was surrounded and threatened by enemies. So he prayed, "O LORD, do not keep silent; O Lord, do not be far from me. Stir up Yourself, and awake to my right and to my cause, my God and my Lord" (Psalm 35:22–23 NASB).

When faced with an even more serious threat later on, David prayed, "To You, O LORD, I call; my rock, do not be deaf to me, for if You are silent to me, I will become like those who go down to the pit" (Psalm 28:1 NASB). This was a life-or-death situation. But despite finding himself in desperate straits and initially feeling anxious about God's lack of response, David declared in the same psalm, "Blessed be the LORD, because He has heard the voice of my supplication. . . . My heart trusts in Him, and I am helped" (vv. 6–7 NASB).

It takes great faith to believe that God has heard your prayers for your children even though there is no visible sign yet that He has. It takes great faith to believe that God will help them when there is no sure indication He's going to do anything. When faced with prolonged testing like this, children give in to discouragement more easily than adults. After all, you have many years of life experience to assure you that God will eventually come through for you—usually after you've learned the lesson He's trying to teach you.

Paul wrote, "We can rejoice, too, when we run into problems and trials, for we know that they help us develop endurance" (Romans 5:3 NLT). But this is a mature attitude, one that even many adults haven't mastered, let alone children. So comfort your children, encourage them, and pray that God will strengthen their faith. Assure them you're praying for them—and that despite the present lack of response, God *does* care and hear their prayers. He will answer in His time and in the way He deems best.

Dear God, I confess it's very difficult for me—as it was for King David—when You give no answer to my many prayers for my children, and even seem to be hiding or turning Your face away. Yet I know this isn't what's actually happening. Your Word assures me that You're loving and that You work all things for good in both my life and theirs (1 John 4:8; Romans 8:28). Give me the right words to communicate these truths to them. Encourage their faith during this time of silence. In Jesus' name I pray. Amen.

FOR FURTHER THOUGHT

- Does God sometimes seem to be silent or hiding Himself from you?
- What good can come of God waiting so long to answer prayers?
- What three things can you do for your child when God seems silent?

33.

Prayer When Your Child Is Sick

At some point in his reign, David became quite sick. Most likely this happened during his last decade. David's enemies were delighted and hoped he would die. Several powerful Israelite leaders had joined Absalom's rebellion, and although they had been defeated and David was still king, they remained his enemies.

David wrote in Psalm 41, "All who hate me whisper together against me; against me they devise my hurt. 'An evil disease,' they say, 'clings to him. And now that he lies down, he will rise up no more' " (Psalm 41:7–8 NKJV). But David declared to God, "You will not deliver him to the will of his enemies. The LORD will strengthen him on his bed of illness; You will sustain him on his sickbed" (vv. 2–3 NKJV).

Despite the circling vultures, David didn't give up but proclaimed, "Depart from me, all you workers of iniquity; for the LORD has heard the voice of my weeping. The LORD has heard my supplication; the LORD will receive my prayer" (Psalm 6:8–9 NKJV). He was old and sick but was confident that God would heal him and keep him on the throne to continue guiding his people. And God did. David recovered and remained Israel's ruler until he died a natural death at age seventy.

Prolonged serious illness will drive you to your knees—and not just your own sicknesses, but those of your children. David fathered many sons, and the Bible tells us what happened when one of them became sick.

David had committed adultery with Bathsheba and she became pregnant. Not long after the child's birth, "the Lord struck the child that Uriah's wife had borne to David, and he became ill. David pleaded with God for the child. He fasted and spent the nights lying in sackcloth on the ground. . . . On the seventh day the child died" (2 Samuel 12:15–16, 18 niv).

In David's case, it was the Lord's will for him to be healed—contingent on his stirring himself up to pray, mind you. But in the case of his son (which admittedly was an unusual circumstance), it was not God's will for the child to live, and God told David this before he started praying. So why did David pray for seven days? Because he knew that God didn't "afflict willingly, nor grieve the children of men" (Lamentations 3:33 nkjv), and he thought, "Who knows? The Lord may be gracious to me and let the child live" (2 Samuel 12:22 niv).

David had seriously sinned, true, but don't forget: he had also fully repented. And think about what a father's heart he manifested! "David pleaded with God for the child" for seven straight days, during which time he fasted and lay prone on the ground. David knew that God's heart and hand were often moved by earnest, sincere prayers. So he prayed.

In the broadest sense, it's usually always within God's will that your children be healed. Very rarely does God determine that a child must die. This is why He gives their bodies amazing self-healing abilities. This is why He often allows doctors and modern medicine to be so effective. And this is why, if you have faith and pray, He frequently heals.

As a mother, you suffer when you see your children

suffer. Even if they aren't in danger of dying, the fact that some disease or accident causes them to be bedridden or greatly restricted touches you in a profound way. You want to see them fully healed. So, besides taking practical steps to bring about their healing, pray. A miracle isn't guaranteed, but who knows? The Lord may be gracious to you.

Father, like King David, I bring before You the health of my children. I pray for my son/daughter who is sick right now. O God, I know You have the power to do a miracle and heal them. I also know You love them and have great compassion on them. So, Lord, I pray that You stretch forth Your hand and heal my child. If it's not Your will to heal them completely, but they must live with physical handicaps, please give them the patience and the courage to be all they can be. In Jesus' name. Amen.

FOR FURTHER THOUGHT

- How difficult is it to accept that God allows some children to heal but not others?
- Why does God sometimes act only if you pray desperately for Him to?

34.

PRAYER FOR GROWN-UP CHILDREN

Things can be so busy during the years that your children are growing up that you don't notice time passing. Then suddenly one day they're graduating from high school, getting jobs, and preparing to leave home. The nest will soon be empty, and like the psalmist says, you will be "like a sparrow alone on the housetop" (Psalm 102:7 NKJV). It's hard to believe your children are now young adults. And it's just as perplexing to ponder your own aging and mortality.

An unknown psalmist prayed:

> *Hear my prayer, O LORD, and let my cry come to You. . . . I lie awake, and am like a sparrow alone on the housetop. . . . I said, "O my God, do not take me away in the midst of my days; Your years are throughout all generations. Of old You laid the foundation of the earth, and the heavens are the work of Your hands. They will perish, but You will endure. . .they will be changed. But You are the same, and Your years will have no end. The children of Your servants will continue, and their descendants will be established before You."*
> *(Psalm 102:1, 7, 24–28 NKJV)*

Like Abraham, your children are obeying God's call: "Abraham obeyed when God called him to leave home and go to another land" (Hebrews 11:8 NLT). So too, your children are about to "leave home and never return" (Job 39:4 NLT).

In Bible times, young men and women normally didn't leave their parents' house until they got married—"Therefore shall a man leave his father and his mother, and shall cleave unto his wife" (Genesis 2:24 KJV)—but these days single young adults often leave long before they marry.

Your job as a parent is almost done. Yes, they'll still need your advice from time to time, they may need a small loan in a pinch, and when the grandchildren come, they'll need a babysitter, but as you watch your last child prepare to leave home, you can almost hear the Lord saying, "Well done, thou good and faithful servant" (Matthew 25:21 KJV).

But perhaps a huge question forms in your mind: "Are they ready?" You wonder if you've trained them well enough. You wonder if they'll achieve their goals and dreams. And even more importantly, will they fulfill God's purpose for their lives? But notice the promise: "The children of Your servants will continue, and their descendants will be established before You' " (Psalm 102:28 NKJV). As long as you have trained them well, and as long as they serve Him, God will establish your children.

Just the same, you can't help but worry a little about them. But the wisest thing you can do is turn any anxious thought into a prayer. Pray that God will bless your children, lead them, and give them courage and wisdom. As you'll soon find out, you're not done praying for them yet—not by a long shot.

The good thing is, you can be confident that the same God who watched over you and your family when your kids were little will continue to watch over them now. He's the everlasting Lord, and He doesn't change. As the psalm above says, "You are the same, and Your years will have no end." God will always be faithful to guide and protect your children as long as they seek Him. And you can join your prayers to theirs.

Dear Lord, my emotions are really mixed right now. On one hand, I feel fulfilled and happy, like a major life's mission has been accomplished. On the other hand, I feel a little sad, missing my kids already. And I'm a little worried. So please go with them, Lord, as they head out into the world. Bless them and protect them, and keep them close to You. Don't let the world derail their faith or steal their optimism. Help me to continue to pray for them, because they'll always be my children even when they're on their own. I commit them into Your hands, dear God. In Jesus' name. Amen.

FOR FURTHER THOUGHT

- What is the "empty nest syndrome"? What emotions do new empty nesters experience?

- How can watching your children leave home bring a fulfilling feeling?

- How can you best pray for your children during this time of transition?

35.

PRAYER IN PROSPEROUS TIMES

As a mother, you want to provide all your kids' needs, and that's a good thing. But when children are completely secure and have their every need supplied, they may live in such a bubble that they take things for granted. As a result, they may fail to realize their dependence on God. They may not even bother to pray. But they definitely need God, whether they think they do or not.

An unknown psalmist prayed, "O Lord my God, how great you are! . . . You cause grass to grow for the livestock and plants for people to use. You allow them to produce food from the earth—wine to make them glad, olive oil to soothe their skin, and bread to give them strength. . . . They all depend on you to give them food as they need it. When you supply it, they gather it. You open your hand to feed them, and they are richly satisfied" (Psalm 104:1, 14–15, 27–28 NLT).

But many people forget that God does all this, so He warned:

> *"Beware that you do not forget the Lord your*
> *God. . .lest—when you have eaten and are full,*
> *and have built beautiful houses and dwell in them;*
> *and when your herds and your flocks multiply, and*
> *your silver and your gold are multiplied, and all*
> *that you have is multiplied. . .then you say in your*
> *heart, 'My power and the might of my hand have*
> *gained me this wealth.'*

*"And you shall remember the L*ORD *your God,*
for it is He who gives you power to get wealth."
*(Deuteronomy 8:11–14, 17–18 N*KJV*)*

The Christians of Laodicea were in this position and declared, "I am rich, have become wealthy, and have need of nothing" (Revelation 3:17 NKJV). You teach your children to pray, "Our Father which art in heaven. . .give us this day our daily bread" (Matthew 6:9, 11 KJV), and they need to keep firmly in their minds the truth that God is indeed the One supplying their needs.

One of the best ways to emphasize your children's dependence on God is to lead them in prayer every day, thanking God for giving them everything they have. Be faithful to pause and pray over your food every time you eat. It may not be dangerous to eat an unblessed hot dog, but remembering to do so gives you one more occasion to remind your kids that God is ultimately the One who supplies everything they have. The prophet Jeremiah wrote, "The LORD is good to those who depend on him" (Lamentations 3:25 NLT).

Teaching your children to tithe at an early age is another way to underscore their dependence on God. It takes faith to give God 10 percent of your money and trust that you'll be able to make it on what's left. The Bible encourages, "Honor the LORD with your wealth, with the firstfruits of all your crops; then your barns will be filled to overflowing" (Proverbs 3:9–10 NIV). Whether you believe in tithing or simply in giving generous offerings, God blesses a commitment to give (2 Corinthians 9:6). And it teaches your children that God owns everything.

Another thing you can do is lead your kids in prayer for children who lack food and other basic necessities.

Many children are living in poverty in countries around the world, and it does your kids good to have their eyes opened to these needs. If this newfound awareness moves them to want to donate to Christian charities, all the better. Help them decide how much of their own money to give. Remind them, "He who has pity on the poor lends to the LORD, and He will pay back what he has given" (Proverbs 19:17 NKJV).

Father in heaven, thank You for providing all our needs and a comfortable lifestyle. I pray that my children won't take the riches of Your bounty for granted or neglect to thank You for all You give us. I pray they'll realize that everything we have ultimately comes from You. Help my children to remember to thank You for all things. Help me to teach them, through both word and example, that You are our Provider. In Jesus' name. Amen.

FOR FURTHER THOUGHT

- How is God your ultimate source of supply, even if you and/or your husband have a steady job?

- What are some ways that children forget that the Lord is their Provider?

- How does giving/tithing prove your children's dependence on God?

36.

Spiritual Sculpting

In Psalm 144 David prays a number of powerful blessings upon the righteous:

> *I will sing a new song to You, O God. . . . Rescue me and deliver me from the hand of foreigners. . . that our sons may be as plants grown up in their youth; that our daughters may be as pillars, sculptured in palace style; that our barns may be full, supplying all kinds of produce; that our sheep may bring forth thousands and ten thousands in our fields; that our oxen may be well laden; that there be no breaking in or going out; that there be no outcry in our streets. Happy are the people who are in such a state; happy are the people whose God is the Lord! (Psalm 144:9, 11–15 NKJV)*

It's clear that David had Deuteronomy 28:1–8 in mind, since all of these same blessings are mentioned there and he practically quotes them. There is much to consider in Deuteronomy's grand symphony of blessings, but for now, focus on God's promise to your children: "It shall come to pass, if you diligently obey the voice of the Lord your God, to observe carefully all His commandments. . . . Blessed shall be the fruit of your body" (Deuteronomy 28:1, 4 NKJV).

A vital part of prayer is having a thankful heart and praising the Lord. Psalm 147 declares the happy state of the righteous and their sons and daughters, saying, "Praise the LORD, O Jerusalem! Praise your God, O Zion! For He has strengthened the bars of your gates; He has blessed your children within you" (Psalm 147:12–13 NKJV). You should pray for your children even if they aren't having problems. What should you pray? Praise the Lord for His many blessings upon them.

In Psalm 144 above, God promises to strengthen your spiritual defenses and bless your children. In another place, He speaks of these same two blessings, saying, "I will make your battlements of rubies, your gates of sparkling jewels, and all your walls of precious stones. All your children will be taught by the LORD, and great will be their peace" (Isaiah 54:12–13 NIV).

Why is their peace great? To paraphrase Psalm 144:15: "Happy are the children who are in such a blessed, protected state, blessed by the prayers of their parents; happy are the children whose God is the LORD!"

Speaking of precious stones, the pillars that upheld royal palaces were usually made of costly marble hewn out of a quarry. All true believers have Abraham as their father (Romans 4:16), and the Lord says in Isaiah 51:1–2 (NKJV), "Listen to Me, you who follow after righteousness, you who seek the LORD: Look to the rock from which you were hewn. . . . Look to Abraham your father."

David refers to daughters being exquisitely "sculptured in palace style" out of precious stone. The King James Version says they're "polished," showing that no expense was spared to highlight their beauty. This is a picture of the careful, loving thought that should go into your children's training.

Some people wonder why Psalm 144 seems to honor daughters far more than sons. David prays that Israelite sons may be as plants, but prays that the daughters may be as pillars. These descriptions reflect where they spent most of their time: most Israelite men labored out in the fields, vineyards, and orchards, among plants, but women mostly worked in and around the house. They were pillars of the home. David likely had his own daughters in mind when he mentioned their being beautiful enough to be in palaces.

You "sculpt" your children by training them, disciplining them, reminding them of God's Word, and—very importantly—praying for them. Sculpt your children well.

Dear Father in heaven, thank You for the beautiful lives You've entrusted to my care. You view my children as very precious stones, but they're not born fully finished or final-formed. You've appointed me to guide their behavior and shape them in their formative years. Help me to be a diligent sculptor, and faithfully direct me to train them the way You would have me to. In Jesus' name I pray. Amen.

FOR FURTHER THOUGHT

- How much careful thought do you put into your children's training?

- How often do you pray God's blessings upon your children?

- What particular sculpting touch do your children need at this time?

- Is God calling you to pray for one of your children in particular?

37.

PRAYER TO BE A GOOD TEACHER

David prayed, "Now also when I am old and grayheaded, O God, do not forsake me, until I declare Your strength to this generation, Your power to everyone who is to come" (Psalm 71:18 NKJV). You may or may not be old and grayheaded, but you can pray this powerful prayer over your own life as well.

When speaking of God's commandments, Moses instructed parents, "You shall teach them diligently to your children, and shall talk of them when you sit in your house, when you walk by the way, when you lie down, and when you rise up" (Deuteronomy 6:7 NKJV). He meant for you to be intentional and focus on your kids' training all day long, every waking moment you spend with them.

If you constantly focus on sharing the Word with your children while making sure that you're "speaking the truth in love" (Ephesians 4:15 KJV), your thoughts and speech will be full of God's life, and your children's lives will be full of blessings and peace.

Of course, God doesn't intend for you to quote scripture to your kids nonstop. Both you and they would burn out quickly on such a concentrated diet. No one wants to be preached at 24-7. The Lord wants you to have downtime, plenty of it, when you relax and simply enjoy being together. But here's the key thought: it's important that you model Christlike behavior to your little ones all the time, even in your jokes and entertainment choices.

It's possible to strike a balance between imparting

instruction and letting your children know that you accept them and love them unconditionally. Paul wrote, "Fathers, do not exasperate your children; instead, bring them up in the training and instruction of the Lord" (Ephesians 6:4 NIV). You not only need to teach them what God's Word says but also must train them and mold their behavior.

Psalm 145 emphasizes the importance of sharing God's Word with your children: "One generation shall praise Your works to another, and shall declare Your mighty acts. I will meditate on the glorious splendor of Your majesty, and on Your wondrous works. Men shall speak of the might of Your awesome acts, and I will declare Your greatness. They shall utter the memory of Your great goodness, and shall sing of Your righteousness" (Psalm 145:4–7 NKJV).

And another psalm says: "He decreed statutes for Jacob and established the law in Israel, which he commanded our ancestors to teach their children, so the next generation would know them, even the children yet to be born, and they in turn would tell their children. Then they would put their trust in God" (Psalm 78:5–7 NIV).

As you teach your children, you want to make sure your delivery is straightforward and natural. You don't want to come across as stern, legalistic, or preachy. So pray that you're able to share the Word in appropriate contexts, in times of humor as well as serious times. Your children need your laughs as much as your lectures.

It's not enough to just sow the seeds of the Word, however. You also need to water them with prayer. Otherwise, the Word might end up like the seed in Jesus' parable that fell on hard, unreceptive hearts on the path, or on rocky ground, or among thorns (Mark 4:3–7 NIV). Pray that your children's hearts become open, soft, and yielding so that God's seeds sink their roots down deep and the cares of this life don't choke them out.

Father in heaven, thank You for Your wonderful Word. Help me to consistently share Your Word with my children. Help me to find new, inventive, appropriate, and even funny ways to share it with them. Help their hearts to be receptive, and bless Your Word as it sends down its roots and becomes an integral part of their lives. In Jesus' name I pray. Amen.

FOR FURTHER THOUGHT

- Why must you snatch moments here and there to share God's Word?
- Why is it important to pray that the Word grows deep in your children's hearts?
- What's the difference between the training and the instruction of the Lord?

38.

DAVID'S PRAYER FOR SOLOMON

David wanted to build a temple for God, but the Lord told him he had waged too many wars and shed too much blood. But God promised that David's son Solomon, who would be a man of peace, would build Him a temple. In his final days, David recounted to the Israelites what God had told him: "It is your son Solomon who shall build My house and My courts; for I have chosen him to be My son, and I will be his Father" (1 Chronicles 28:6 NKJV).

After the Israelites had given much gold and silver for the building project, David prayed publicly, "O LORD our God, all this abundance that we have prepared to build You a house for Your holy name is from Your hand, and is all Your own. I know also, my God, that You test the heart and have pleasure in uprightness. . . . Give my son Solomon a loyal heart to keep Your commandments and Your testimonies and Your statutes, to do all these things, and to build the temple for which I have made provision" (1 Chronicles 29:16–17, 19 NKJV).

When your children's gifts and talents begin to become obvious, when specific desires and visions stir in their hearts and they start to apply themselves to their future calling, be diligent to pray for them. David prayed not only that his son would fulfill one of his major life missions by building God's temple but also—and very importantly—that God would give him a loyal heart. After all, without a deep love for the Lord, all passion is pointless and all talent is worthless.

Then David informed Solomon, "As for you, my son Solomon, know the God of your father, and serve Him with a loyal heart and with a willing mind; for the LORD searches all hearts and understands all the intent of the thoughts. If you seek Him, He will be found by you; but if you forsake Him, He will cast you off forever. Consider now, for the LORD has chosen you to build a house for the sanctuary; be strong, and do it" (1 Chronicles 28:9–10 NKJV).

David already knew that Solomon would build the temple, but he may have wondered why God stressed that Solomon should be true to Him. As it turned out, this was no mere formality. Although neither David nor his son knew it at the time, Solomon would be greatly tempted in his later years to forsake the Lord. So God impressed the need for faithfulness on David's heart. When you pray for your children, God will frequently lead you to pray words that offer specific insight and guidance, even if the reason isn't immediately apparent.

God was a Father to Solomon just as He is to you and your children today. He promises, "I will be a Father to you, and you shall be My sons and daughters" (2 Corinthians 6:18 NKJV). To be a child of God is a tremendous privilege, but it also requires deep commitment and the forsaking of worldly values. The verse right before this one says, "Come out from among them and be separate, says the Lord. Do not touch what is unclean, and I will receive you" (v. 17 NKJV).

God calls your children to serve Him with willing minds and to be resolved and strong in what they do for Him. Young children often don't understand what perseverance means, hanging on in both fair times and hard times, but they can certainly understand what it means to have a good attitude. If they will continually have a willing heart, perseverance will come naturally over time. Pray that the virtues of commitment and perseverance will grow in your children's hearts.

Dear God, thank You that You are a Father to me and to my children, just like You were to Solomon. Give me a heart that is loyal to You, and help me to be faithful to You at all times. May I model a passionate, steady love for You. Help my children to be true to You. Help them not to turn away from You, even in temporary coldness or disinterest. And thank You that You care greatly for my children and have a wonderful plan for their lives. May they fulfill Your will for them and accomplish all that You have ordained for them. In Jesus' name I pray. Amen.

FOR FURTHER THOUGHT

- God said He would be a Father to Solomon. What did that mean?

- What are the specific gifts and callings of each of your children?

- What weaknesses might derail your children from their goals?

- God searches and tests hearts. What do these tests look like?

39.

PRAYING FOR WISDOM

Shortly after Solomon became king, he went to Gibeon to sacrifice to God. That night the Lord appeared to him in a dream and said, "Ask what you wish Me to give you" (1 Kings 3:5 NASB). This is the only time in the Bible when God offered to give a person whatever they asked for, and Solomon could have requested many things for his personal benefit.

But Solomon prayed, "O LORD my God, You have made Your servant king in place of my father David, yet I am but a little child; I do not know how to go out or come in. Your servant is in the midst of Your people which You have chosen, a great people who are too many to be numbered or counted. So give Your servant an understanding heart to judge Your people to discern between good and evil. For who is able to judge this great people of Yours?" (vv. 7–9 NASB).

Solomon was apparently a young man of average intelligence before this, and having just ascended to the throne, he was overwhelmed with feelings of inadequacy. He wasn't looking forward to the responsibility of making a constant stream of difficult decisions. Shortly before this, David, when dying, had brought up the need to render justice to Joab and had told Solomon, "Therefore do according to your wisdom" (1 Kings 2:6 NKJV). And regarding Shimei, David said, "Do not hold him guiltless, for you are a wise man and know what you ought to do to him" (v. 9 NKJV).

But the problem was, Solomon *didn't* know what he ought to do—especially with Shimei, to whom David had sworn that he wouldn't die (2 Samuel 19:21–23). He felt his own decision-making abilities were woefully inadequate. So he asked God for a download of supernatural wisdom in order to make good decisions.

Paul also was faced with perplexing choices at times. He wrote, "What I shall choose I cannot tell. For I am hard-pressed between the two, having a desire to depart and be with Christ, which is far better. Nevertheless to remain in the flesh is more needful for you." Then, hit by divine inspiration, he added, "And being confident of this, I know that I shall remain and continue with you all for your progress and joy of faith" (Philippians 1:22–25 NKJV).

Like Solomon, your children will face difficult decisions in their adult lives, and they'll need the supernatural wisdom of the Lord to help them. In fact, they sometimes face hard choices even now. The good news is, God is still delighted to give His children wisdom. The Bible promises, "If any of you lacks wisdom, let him ask of God, who gives to all generously and without reproach, and it will be given to him" (James 1:5 NASB).

God loves to give other spiritual gifts as well. Paul wrote that believers are to seek wisdom. "Wisdom is the principal thing; therefore get wisdom" (Proverbs 4:7 NKJV). The Bible says we are to "earnestly desire the best gifts" (1 Corinthians 12:31 NKJV). And we know that "a spiritual gift is given to each of us so we can help each other" (1 Corinthians 12:7 NLT). This, of course, was the very reason Solomon asked for wisdom.

Solomon was a young man a little over twenty when

he became king, but he prayed, "I am but a little child." He recognized that God was his Father, the source of all wisdom, and the only One who could give him insight, wisdom, and knowledge. So like a trusting child, he turned to his Father for help. As a parent, you're often required to make important decisions on behalf of your children, and like Solomon and Paul, you may not know what to do. That's when you must pray and depend on God to make things clear to you.

Dear Father, help me to make wise choices in matters that concern my children. It's often difficult to know what the right choice is, so I ask You to send Your Holy Spirit to give me insight and wisdom. Sometimes the choices seem so similar that it's hard to know what to do. Other times, I know what's right, but I'm tempted to take the easy way out. So help me, please. And I pray that You help my children as they make choices based on what Your Word says. In Jesus' name I pray. Amen.

FOR FURTHER THOUGHT

- Why is making decisions so difficult sometimes?
- How can God's Spirit make the right choice clear to you?
- How can decisions made in childhood have consequences for all life?

40.

PRAYERS BORN OF GRIEF

Believers sometimes pray prayers born of pain. When children get sick, have an accident, or are betrayed, they may ask their parents in an accusing tone, "*Why* did God let this happen?" And if a loved one dies, their grief is even keener, as is their disappointment with God. They may express strong emotions when praying.

You will probably assure them that God is good, even if they can't understand some of the things He allows. It helps to have a heart-to-heart talk with them to explain the issues and defuse their anger. But don't just tell your child—especially a teen—that they're *wrong* to be angry. If they simply bottle up their anger inside without resolving it, it can easily turn into a simmering hatred, and then they may stop praying altogether because they're no longer on speaking terms with God.

One time, during a drought, the Lord instructed Elijah to go to a village in Phoenicia and stay with a widow and her son. God miraculously provided food for them, and the widow was grateful. But after a time, her son became sick, grew worse and worse, and finally died. The widow wailed, "O man of God, what have you done to me? Have you come here to point out my sins and kill my son?" (1 Kings 17:18 NLT).

Elijah took the dead boy, carried him to his room, and laid him on his bed. He was in anguish, partly because the widow had accused him of being responsible for her son's death. So he cried out, "O LORD my God, why have you brought tragedy to this widow who has opened her home to me, causing her son to die?" Elijah wondered if God had acted unfairly. Then he prayed, "O LORD my God, please let this child's life return to him" (vv. 20–21 NLT).

Elijah didn't accuse God of wrongdoing. He stuck to the facts: God had indeed allowed the boy to die. And despite his anguish, Elijah knew that God was good and twice called Him "O LORD my God." Then "the LORD heard Elijah's prayer" (v. 22 NLT) and the child came back to life.

When your children or other loved ones suffer tragedy, your emotions become fully engaged and color your prayers. Read the Psalms and see how David uttered deeply emotional prayers, questioning God. The following prayer is probably stronger than anything you'd normally pray: "Arouse Yourself, why do You sleep, O Lord? Awake, do not reject us forever. Why do You hide Your face and forget our affliction and our oppression?" (Psalm 44:23–24 NASB). Accusing God of sleeping? Of forgetting pain and oppression? Those are strong words.

Several thousand years later you can still feel the heat from this prayer. And while you might explain that David was using metaphorical language and wasn't literally accusing God, still, it's not a prayer you'd hear from the pulpit. You've probably prayed one or two prayers like that in your lifetime. Yes, believers sometimes pray such words. But God knows they come from lives overflowing with grief. He's aware that mortals often can't understand what He's doing, so He listens past the confusion and anger to the sincere cry to Him. Of course, God prefers that people *not* accuse Him, since doing so is a sin. Even though Job suffered greatly, "Job did not sin by charging God with wrongdoing" (Job 1:22 NIV). At least not at first. Later he *did* loudly and repeatedly accuse God of unfairly afflicting him, so much so that he had to confess, "I spoke of things I did not understand," and said, "Therefore I. . .repent" (Job 42:3, 6 NIV). If you or your children accuse God in a time of pain or grief, then after the crisis is past, He will remind you of your rash words and of your need to repent of them.

Father in heaven, thank You that You have the love and the wisdom to see past my childish attitudes and immature prayers. So many of my prayers for my children are half-formed, poorly-thought-out things. I cry out in anger when You allow them to get sick. I pray in frustration when You're slow to change their bad habits. I complain to You when they act stubborn and willful. Thank You for hearing and answering my poor prayers just the same, and for forgiving my anger. In Jesus' name I pray. Amen.

FOR FURTHER THOUGHT

- Have you ever prayed an accusatory prayer? What happened as a result?

- Why does God allow bad things to happen to good people?

- Does God intend that your emotions become engaged when praying?

41.

FERVENT, REPEATED PRAYERS

Often when praying for your children, you may be mystified as to why certain prayers are answered almost instantly, while it seems to take forever to get an answer to others. You may wonder whether the apparent lack of a response is God's way of saying no. When this happens, many people eventually give up and stop praying. So why does God withhold a response sometimes?

At the beginning of his ministry, "Elijah. . .prayed earnestly that it would not rain; and it did not rain on the land for three years and six months" (James 5:17 NKJV). But after God sent down fire on Mount Carmel to prove He was the true God, it was time for the drought to end. So Elijah climbed to the top of the mountain, bowed down, and prayed. Then he said to his servant, "Go up now, look toward the sea." His servant went but came back saying, "There is nothing."

Seven times Elijah repeated, "Go again." Finally, his servant came back and reported, "There is a cloud, as small as a man's hand, rising out of the sea!" Within minutes, a strong storm system blew in from the sea, turning the entire sky black. Along with it came wind and a heavy rain (1 Kings 18:41–45 NKJV).

Elijah had prayed for a drought, and it didn't rain for years. "He prayed again, and the heaven gave rain" (James 5:18 NKJV). While it's true that Elijah had tremendous faith, the same power of God is available to believers today. After all, "Elijah was a man with a nature like ours"

(v. 17 NKJV). Christians just need to pray fervently. "The effective, fervent prayer of a righteous man avails much" (v. 16 NKJV).

Moreover, you often need to bring a request to the Lord many times. It took multiple requests before God sent rain. Why then did God send down fire after Elijah prayed one brief prayer? (See 1 Kings 18:36–38.) Well, consider this: although Elijah prayed only a short prayer on Mount Carmel, he *had* been praying every day for 1,277 days (three and a half years) leading up to this moment—and most likely had been praying continually for the same thing: for God to show His power so the people would know that He was God. All the pent-up power was released in one dramatic instant.

This brings out a thought that most mothers don't particularly like: God often requires you to pray day after day for months—sometimes even years—to bring about changes in your child. Perhaps it's a certain genre of worldly music your teen listens to, or the statements your daughter is making by her clothing, or your son's total lack of interest in reading the Bible or attending church. Or perhaps certain friends influence your children negatively. God wants you to bring these matters to Him in prayer—not just once, but time after time.

Jesus said, "When you pray, do not keep on babbling like pagans, for they think they will be heard because of their many words" (Matthew 6:7 NIV). The pagan Romans were known for their formulaic, ritualized, but empty prayers. Jesus wasn't discouraging Christians from praying repeatedly to God for the same desperate need. Heartfelt, sincere prayers aren't "babbling."

You may ask, "Why would God want to hear similar

prayers every day for so long? What is the point of that? Why doesn't He do a miracle after just one prayer?" One of the main reasons God requires repeated prayers is that they do much-needed work in your *own* life. For one, they demonstrate your love and concern. Moreover, delayed answers, despite seeming like denial, teach you perseverance, patience, and unfailing trust.

When asked how God did a miracle to bring them back to Him, many prodigal teens have testified the same thing: "My parents *never stopped praying* for me."

God, I ask You to forgive me for being impatient in my prayer life. I've wanted You to fit into my busy schedule and for prayer to be quick, like the drive-through at a fast-food restaurant. I thank You that You're working not only in my child's life but in my life as well. I thank You that You will answer my prayers even if it takes time. Please help me to continue to trust You and to be patient. In Jesus' name I pray. Amen.

FOR FURTHER THOUGHT

- Why are some prayers answered instantly, while responses to others come more slowly?
- Why does God sometimes require you to pray for years for the same thing?
- What changes does God want you to pray for in your child's life?

42.

OPEN THEIR EYES, LORD

When the king of Aram was at war with Israel, he would say to his officers, "We will mobilize our forces at such and such a place." But Elisha the prophet of God would warn the king of Israel not to go near that place. Time and again Elisha warned him. Enraged, the king of Aram demanded of his officers, "Who has been informing the king of Israel of my plans?" An officer replied, "It's not us. . . . Elisha, the prophet in Israel, tells the king of Israel even the words you speak in the privacy of your bedroom!"

"Go and find out where he is," the king ordered. Soon they reported back: "Elisha is at Dothan." So during the night the king of Aram sent a great army with many chariots and horses to surround the city. When Elisha's servant got up early the next morning, he looked off the wall and saw troops, horses, and chariots all around the city. "What will we do now?" he cried.

"Don't be afraid!" Elisha told him. "For there are more on our side than on theirs!" When the servant gave him a blank look, Elisha prayed, "O LORD, open his eyes and let him see!" God opened the servant's spiritual eyes, and he saw that the hillside around them was filled with horses and chariots of fire. Then Elisha prayed, "O LORD, please make them blind." So the Lord struck the Arameans with blindness (2 Kings 6:8–18 NLT). They couldn't *see* Elisha, so they eventually went back to Aram without him. There's more to the story than that, but that's what it came down to.

You probably wish God would answer *your* prayers like that and let you have such insight into behind-the-scenes happenings. But the reason Elisha was able to pray such short, direct public prayers and receive immediate answers was that he'd done a great deal of private praying beforehand. He *lived* in the supernatural realm, in close contact with God, and he was in constant prayer all day long, so the Lord revealed amazing things to him and answered his prayers in amazing ways.

You may have concluded, however, that you can't pray so much, even if it means having a powerful connection with God. Yet even if you're super busy, you can still keep your heart focused on the Lord. God promises, "Because he has set his love upon Me. . .he shall call upon Me, and I will answer him" (Psalm 91:14–15 NKJV).

Perhaps you wish your children would learn basic social skills like getting along with their brothers and sisters without quarreling and fighting. Continual reminders reinforced with discipline go a long way toward getting this message through to them, but in the end, if they're truly to understand, the Lord will have to open the eyes of their hearts. Otherwise they'll only behave when you're present and revert to their default behavior the moment you step out of the room.

Or perhaps you long for your children to grasp basic truths about God—the fact that He's real, or that He loves them, or that He will protect them. If so, you can pray, "Lord, open their eyes!" God calls you to do your part: you must set an example of godly behavior; you must teach His Word to your children; you must discipline them; and you must pray for them. If you do these things, God will be faithful to do His part, the things you *can't* do: He will cause them to grasp that He really exists, that He loves and cares for them, and that He has a wonderful plan for their lives.

Paul wrote, "I pray that the eyes of your heart may be enlightened in order that you may know the hope to which he has called you, the riches of his glorious inheritance" (Ephesians 1:18 NIV). If you pray, your children's eyes will be opened and God will be able to enlighten them by His Holy Spirit.

Dear Lord, I pray that You'll do a miracle and open my children's eyes to see that You are real, that You live inside their hearts, and that You're with them every moment of every day. May they truly love You and know You, Lord. Help them also to understand with their hearts that You love them and are working all circumstances for their good. In Jesus' name I pray. Amen.

FOR FURTHER THOUGHT

- Have there been times when God miraculously enlightened you to a truth?
- What are you praying for God to open your children's eyes to see?
- Why can discipline and training take your kids only so far toward God?

43.

OBEYING AND PRAYING

Sailors often have reason to pray. "Those who go down to the sea in ships. . .see the works of the LORD. . . . He commands and raises the stormy wind, which lifts up the waves of the sea. . . . Then they cry out to the LORD in their trouble, and He brings them out of their distresses. He calms the storm" (Psalm 107:23–25, 28–29 NKJV).

In Jonah's day, some sailors found themselves in this exact situation. God had told Jonah to go to Nineveh and warn the people there of His coming judgment, but Jonah refused. Instead, he fled in the opposite direction, to Tarshish (southern Spain), at the western end of the known world. As they began sailing, the Lord sent a great wind to batter the ship. The sailors cried to their gods and woke Jonah, saying, "Call on your God; perhaps your God will consider us, so that we may not perish" (Jonah 1:6 NKJV). But God wasn't listening to Jonah's prayers, because he was stubbornly disobeying.

After confessing what he'd done, Jonah told the sailors, "Pick me up and throw me into the sea" (v. 12 NKJV). At first, the sailors tried everything they could to avoid doing that, but when nothing else worked, they reluctantly tossed Jonah overboard—and immediately the sea ceased raging.

Then the sailors feared God greatly and prayed to Him. The Lord heard the pagan sailors' prayers, but He wasn't listening to Jonah—at least not with intent to answer. "Surely the arm of the LORD is not too short to save, nor his ear too dull to hear. But. . .your sins have hidden his face from you, so that he will not hear" (Isaiah 59:1–2 NIV). This principle applies even to children, which is one reason parents read them the story of Jonah over and over to make sure they understand the lesson: "Don't be a Jonah!" Don't rebel. Don't disobey.

This scenario is even more likely to be played out in the lives of older children and teens. It's normal for teens to seek greater independence in preparation for heading out on their own. But if they're becoming rebellious and disrespectful, they're setting themselves up for trouble, because God may refuse to answer their prayers until they get their hearts right. So pray that the Lord would soften their hearts and get through to them.

Now, teens will have days when they're moody, sullen, and on edge. Part of this irritability is due to all the hormones being released in their bodies. And some kids are just naturally strong-willed. But these are not excuses for outright rebellion and disobedience.

John wrote, "Beloved, if our heart does not condemn us, we have confidence toward God. And whatever we ask we receive from Him, because we keep His commandments and do those things that are pleasing in His sight" (1 John 3:21–22 NKJV). Your heart will condemn you when you're disobeying God, and you won't have confidence that He hears you. But the good news is, if you're doing your best to keep His commandments and please Him, you can have faith that He *will* answer your prayers.

You probably wish your children would never disobey you but would always obey eagerly and cheerfully. But life usually doesn't work out that smoothly, and very likely you'll have to deal with rebellion—at least passive rebellion—at one time or another. Just make sure to pray for wisdom and strength to deal with it. You'll need to be firm, but you'll also need to be sensitive to God's Spirit to know what approach will work best with your child.

Dear Father, I bring my children before You in prayer and ask You to have mercy on them. They've become argumentative, sullen, and rebellious in recent days, and I'm concerned for them. Please soften their hearts and help them to be sensitive to Your Spirit so that they won't have to suffer Your chastisement. Help them to seek You and resolve any issues that stand between You and them so that You can once again hear their prayers and bless them. In Jesus' name I pray. Amen.

FOR FURTHER THOUGHT

- In what ways have your children behaved like Jonah?
- Does God still punish His wayward children? What might He do?
- How can your teens have confidence that God will answer their prayers?

44.

A POTTER'S PRAYERS

Isaiah prayed to God, "You have hidden Your face from us, and have consumed us because of our iniquities. But now, O LORD, You are our Father; we are the clay, and You our potter; and all we are the work of Your hand. Do not be furious, O LORD, nor remember iniquity forever; indeed, please look—we all are Your people!" (Isaiah 64:7–9 NKJV).

The prophet prayed these words during a time of trouble and affliction, when God was punishing His people. But Isaiah looked beyond the troubled times into the heart of God. He believed the Lord deeply loved His people and—despite His present punishment—had good things planned for them. The most important takeaway from this passage is that God is your heavenly Father. Both you and your children are the work of His hand, and you're all works in progress. You're not finished, and neither has He given up on you.

When Jeremiah visited the potter's house (Jeremiah 18:1–11), he observed that the potter found a flaw in the still-moist pot, but by applying steady, firm pressure with his hands, he reworked the yielding clay into a better shape. God then declared, "Behold, like the clay in the potter's hand, so are you in My hand, O house of Israel" (Jeremiah 18:6 NASB).

Now, some people have the idea that it's desirable to be "broken." Yes, David said, "The LORD is close to the brokenhearted and saves those who are crushed in spirit"

(Psalm 34:18 NIV). However, He's near you because He has compassion on you and wants to resolve your troubles and comfort you—not because His goal is to make you broken.

Throughout the scriptures, being broken implies being shattered in judgment with no hope of being put back together (Jeremiah 19:1–2, 10–11). Brokenness implies uselessness (Psalm 31:12) and weakness (Proverbs 15:13; 17:22). It is a judgment on dry, brittle, hardened vessels that can no longer be changed. In contrast, pressure, molding, and reshaping are for vessels that are still soft and moist, still on the potter's wheel, and for which there is hope of change. That's why the Bible says, "Do not harden your hearts" (Psalm 95:8 NKJV).

Just as God, your heavenly Father, is a potter, so also He wants you, as a parent, to be a potter. He wants you to shape your children's lives when they're young and pliable—just as a potter is able to form clay when it's still soft and moist. Often you'll apply the pressure that molds them through discipline: "All discipline for the moment seems not to be joyful, but sorrowful; yet to those who have been trained by it, afterwards it yields the peaceful fruit of righteousness" (Hebrews 12:11 NASB).

Molding also comes through hardship and affliction. Paul said, "We are hard-pressed on every side, yet not crushed; we are perplexed, but not in despair" (2 Corinthians 4:8 NKJV). Believers often are "hard-pressed" because God is using that hard pressure to mold them. However, people are broken when instead of softening and yielding to the pressure, they harden their hearts and resist it. The key is to yield, trust God, and go with the process.

Children are the same. Willful sons and daughters

receive discipline and time-outs. But the big difference between children and clay is that even after children have hardened into an unacceptable shape, God can soften them once again and mold them anew. Still, it's best to shape your children when they're young and most pliable.

A mother's prayers have a powerful effect on her children's lives, keeping their consciences sensitive and receptive to the voice of God. And if your children remain responsive to your words of guidance and correction, they will grow up into sons and daughters who glorify God and bring honor to your family.

> *Lord, I pray that my children will be like moist, yielding clay that can be formed into vessels of excellence. Make their hearts tender and receptive to Your Spirit. Let them be compliant and responsive to my correction. And please give me love and patience so that I discipline them and reshape them with love. I pray that You will have Your perfect will in their lives and mold them into the godly men and women You desire them to become. In the name of Jesus I pray. Amen.*

FOR FURTHER THOUGHT

- Are your children's hearts like soft, pliable clay, or are they hard and brittle?

- How can God soften your children's hearts in answer to your prayers?

- Do you wish to be "broken"? Do you wish your children to be "broken"?

- Do you discipline your child in impatience and anger, or in love and gentleness?

45.

GRATEFUL PRAYERS, NOT LAMENTS

Watching the news can be painful when it highlights the suffering of children in war-torn nations or regions plagued by famine. You see the despair on the faces of the parents who are unable to provide for or protect their children, and it strikes a chord deep within you, for you too are a parent, and one of your deepest fears is that circumstances beyond your control will cause you to fail your children.

The Jews suffered greatly during the Babylonian invasion: Jerusalem was besieged and sacked, famine was widespread, and children starved. In the midst of this horror, Jeremiah called his people to repentance and intercessory prayer. "The hearts of the people cry out to the Lord. . . . Arise, cry out in the night, as the watches of the night begin; pour out your heart like water in the presence of the Lord. Lift up your hands to him for the lives of your children, who faint from hunger at every street corner" (Lamentations 2:18–19 NIV).

It might have seemed hopeless to pray. After all, God's wrath was being visited upon the nation for their sins. He was ignoring their prayers (Jeremiah 7:16; 11:11, 14). So why pray? Why hope for mercy? Yet God's eye was upon the righteous and their children, so Jeremiah said, "I called on your name, LORD, from the depths of the pit. You heard my plea: 'Do not close your ears to my cry for relief.' You came near when I called you, and you said, 'Do not fear' " (Lamentations 3:55–57 NIV).

When you pray to God, you need to be confident that

He will hear your prayers. Sometimes you might doubt this even at the best of times—let alone during a national disaster or judgment. Yet God hears even then and mercifully answers. "For no one is cast off by the Lord forever. Though he brings grief, he will show compassion, so great is his unfailing love. For he does not willingly bring affliction or grief to anyone" (Lamentations 3:31–33 NIV).

God calls you to pray for your children and to trust that He, as their loving heavenly Father, cares for them and will provide for them. The psalmist declared, "I have never seen the godly abandoned or their children begging for bread" (Psalm 37:25 NLT). That doesn't mean you and your children won't face difficult times or will never have to do without anything, but it does mean that God is watching over you and will provide for you.

If you can afford to donate to alleviate the suffering of children in impoverished or war-torn nations, you certainly should do so. Solomon prayed, "May he defend the afflicted among the people and save the children of the needy" (Psalm 72:4 NIV). God often uses people's generosity to accomplish His work. But even if your cash is tight, looking at all the grief and calamity in the world ought to make you very grateful that you live in a land of peace and plenty, and that your children are safe and provided for.

You may not be able to provide everything your kids want and need, and you may wonder where the cash will come from to take care of their dental needs or special lessons, but God has provided thus far and will continue to provide. And even if you have to tell your children no when they make certain requests, because the cash simply isn't there, both you and they still have much to be thankful for. And you *should* be thankful.

Many parents tend to pray only when there's an emergency or a pressing need. Don't let that be you! Remember to praise God for your many blessings, "giving thanks always for all things unto God and the Father" (Ephesians 5:20 KJV).

Dear Lord, thank You that we live in a land of peace and plenty, that despite any hardships or lack, our family is sufficiently provided for. Thank You that my children go to bed at night safe and well fed. Lord, I'm truly grateful. And I want to let You know that I trust You to provide the money to take care of any outstanding needs my children have. You are their God, and You love them even more than I do. So I commit them into Your loving hands. In Jesus' name I pray. Amen.

FOR FURTHER THOUGHT

- In what ways are children in other nations suffering right now?
- Do you trust that God will provide for your children's outstanding needs?
- Despite any financial problems, what are you grateful for?

46.

PRAYING FOR FINANCES

When the Babylonians conquered Jerusalem, many thousands of Jews were slain. Those who survived became slaves, and even young boys were forced to work hard all day long, carrying heavy loads. Jeremiah prayed for their predicament:

> *Remember, O LORD, what has come upon us;*
> *look, and behold our reproach! Our inheritance*
> *has been turned over to aliens, and our houses to*
> *foreigners. We have become orphans and waifs. . . .*
> *Young men ground at the millstones; boys staggered*
> *under loads of wood. . . . Why do You forget us*
> *forever, and forsake us for so long a time? Turn*
> *us back to You, O LORD, and we will be restored.*
> *(Lamentations 5:1–3, 13, 20–21 NKJV)*

Even after the Jews returned from Babylon, many of them still weren't free. There was a drought in Judah, and the poor had to borrow money from wealthier Jews to buy food and pay their taxes to the Persian rulers. Many were forced to surrender the titles to their lands and even to sell their children into slavery to survive. They cried out:

> *"We have mortgaged our fields, vineyards, and*
> *homes to get food during the famine. . . . We have*
> *had to borrow money on our fields and vineyards*
> *to pay our taxes. We belong to the same family as*
> *those who are wealthy, and our children are just*

like theirs. Yet we must sell our children into slavery
just to get enough money to live. We have already
sold some of our daughters, and we are helpless to do
anything about it, for our fields and vineyards are
already mortgaged to others." (Nehemiah 5:3–5 NLT)

How painful it was for parents to see their children work as slaves! Unfortunately, child slavery is still rampant today. According to the latest figures, over 200 million children around the world are being forced to work without wages under harsh circumstances, with no hope of ever becoming free. Yes, you read that right: there are over 200 million *child slaves* in the world today.

Although you can be thankful your children aren't suffering to that extent, you can empathize if you work hard to support them but just barely manage to get by, so your kids must do without certain things; or if you aren't able to finance your teens' ongoing education, so they're forced to take on student loans. There's nothing wrong with being obliged to do hard work, but to a large degree, gone are the days when hard work alone guaranteed a good lifestyle, or when pursuing a degree guaranteed your children secure finances or employment in their chosen field.

So you must regularly commit your finances to God in prayer, because He can bless your finances so that you're able to provide for your children's needs. Here are two promises you can claim when you pray: "Remember the LORD your God, for it is he who gives you the ability to produce wealth" (Deuteronomy 8:18 NIV). "My God will meet all your needs according to the riches of his glory in Christ Jesus" (Philippians 4:19 NIV).

At times you may get tired of petitioning God to bolster your ever-insufficient finances. You might resent the fact that you must pray repeatedly for God to supply the money you need. Why, you wonder, doesn't He just do a big miracle and let you win the lottery? Or why doesn't He simply bless the work of your hands so that you never lack? But God often keeps His children closely dependent on Him because He knows it is the best way to ensure that they'll pray.

So pray! Commit your finances completely to God in prayer, and don't give up. God hears you. He's not ignoring you. He just wants you to come to Him often.

Father in heaven, here I am, coming to You again over my family's finances. I know You're willing to provide, but You also like me close to You and dependent on You. I acknowledge that You're my Provider, and I know You love my children even more than I do. I pray that You'll bless my finances so I can provide for them—not spoil them with abundance, but simply provide their needs. Thank You for the finances I already have. In Jesus' name. Amen.

FOR FURTHER THOUGHT

- What financial needs do you need to pray about right now?

- How can you provide for your children so they aren't burdened later in life?

- How can you avoid being frustrated over continually praying for finances?

47.

PRAISE FOR GOD'S WORD

Around 450 BC during the reign of the Persian Empire, a poor Jewish scribe, rich in faith, penned a most inspiring psalm. His lengthy prayer, written as an acrostic poem, extols the worth and the power of God's Word. Here are just a few verses from his prayer:

> *I have hidden your word in my heart, that I might not sin against you. I praise you, O LORD; teach me your decrees. . . . How I delight in your commands! How I love them! I honor and love your commands. I meditate on your decrees. . . . I think about them all day long. . . . I pray with all my heart; answer me, LORD! I will obey your decrees. . . . I rejoice in your word like one who discovers a great treasure. . . . Those who love your instructions have great peace and do not stumble. (Psalm 119:11–12, 47–48, 97, 145, 162, 165 NLT)*

About one thousand years earlier, Moses had commanded the Israelites, "Take to your heart all the words with which I am warning you today, which you shall command your sons to observe carefully, even all the words of this law. For it is not an idle word for you; indeed it is your life" (Deuteronomy 32:46–47 NASB). They were to teach their children to carefully observe God's words because those words were their very life.

Jesus said, "It is the Spirit who gives life. . .the words that I have spoken to you are spirit and are life" (John 6:63

NASB). This is why God's words give life: they are spiritual and the Spirit of God is full to overflowing with life. That's one reason why Bible reading is so important and why you should love the Word.

"I will obey your decrees," declared the author of Psalm 119 (v. 145 NLT). But the only way to obey them is to know what they say. This is why you spend time in daily devotions. This is why many parents read Bible stories to their children from a very young age and seek to fill their minds with God's Word. As the psalmist said, "I meditate on your decrees. . . . I think about them all day long" (vv. 48, 97 NLT).

Sometimes your older children might not feel like reading the Bible. They might feel like they already know it. But they can constantly learn new things from it. And if they memorize key promises, they'll be able to quote them in times of need or crisis and receive great comfort.

God has given many instructions in the Bible that, if your children follow them, will bring His protection over their lives. "Those who love your instructions have great peace," we read in Psalm 119:165 (NLT). If your kids have a genuine love for the scriptures, they'll have great peace even during trying times.

As a parent, you could hardly do a more important service for your children than giving them a love for God's Word and teaching them to hide it in their hearts. "I have hidden your word in my heart, that I might not sin against you" (v. 11 NLT). And as your kids grow into preteens, it's a good idea to require that they spend time reading their Bible every day, even if they find it boring some days.

Yes, sometimes your children may be tempted to zone out while reading, so pray that God will open the eyes of their spirit to see and understand the Bible's truths. "Open my eyes that I may see wonderful things in your law" (Psalm 119:18 NIV). God can answer this short prayer wonderfully, and He delights to open the hearts of your children to His Word. He can ignite their understanding and comprehension through His Spirit, just like He did for His first disciples. "They said to one another, 'Did not our heart burn within us while He talked with us on the road, and while He opened the Scriptures to us?' " (Luke 24:32 NKJV).

Heavenly Father, thank You for the scriptures that give us spiritual life by introducing us directly to You. I pray that I'll be able to say like that faithful scribe that I honor Your Word and obey it. Help me to be an example to my children of loving and meditating on the truths of the Bible. Help me to commit its promises to memory so that my children will be inspired to do the same. Help me to live its truths so that my children will be able to see a living example of obedience. In Jesus' name I pray. Amen.

FOR FURTHER THOUGHT

- How does God's Word give your children spiritual life?
- Why is it important to fill your children's hearts with scripture?
- Do your children have some key Bible verses memorized?

48.

PRAYING FOR FAVOR FOR YOUR CHILD

Thousands of years ago in Susa, Persia, a Jew named Ne-hemiah was cupbearer to the king. One day his brother arrived from distant Judah, and after the greetings, one of the first questions Nehemiah asked was how their fellow Jews were doing. Unfortunately, his brother answered, "Those who survived the exile. . .are in great trouble and disgrace. The wall of Jerusalem is broken down, and its gates have been burned with fire" (Nehemiah 1:3 NIV).

Nehemiah was hit so hard by this news that he mourned and fasted for several days. Then he prayed:

> "LORD, the God of heaven, the great and awesome
> God, who keeps his covenant of love with those who
> love him and keep his commandments, let your ear
> be attentive and your eyes open to hear the prayer
> your servant is praying before you day and night
> for your servants, the people of Israel. . . . Lord, let
> your ear be attentive to the prayer of this your ser-
> vant and to the prayer of your servants who delight
> in revering your name. Give your servant success
> today by granting him favor in the presence of this
> man [Artaxerxes]." (vv. 5–6, 11 NIV)

The next time Nehemiah saw the king, he informed Ar-taxerxes that his ancestral city was in ruins, so the king asked, "What is it you want?" (2:4 NIV). Nehemiah asked that he be given a leave of absence to go rebuild Jerusalem. The king was pleased to grant this request, so Nehemiah asked for official letters to the local governors to provide him with safe conduct, and a letter to the official in charge of the forests to give him timber. Artaxerxes granted all these requests.

The apostle Paul wrote, "When I became a man, I did away with childish things." Yet he once treasured childish fun, for he admitted, "When I was a child, I used to speak like a child, think like a child, reason like a child" (1 Corinthians 13:11 NASB). One of the greatest blessings for the people of Israel would be to see "the streets of the city. . .filled with boys and girls at play" (Zechariah 8:5 NLT).

When your children are little, you take them to theme parks and playgrounds with swings, teeter-totters, and slides. You'd never go to these places by yourself, but you're happy to drive your children there and watch them play, glad you can facilitate all their fun. The same is true with older children and teens: you frequently drive them to gatherings, parties, or movies that you have zero interest in. But they do, so you put forth the effort to make these things happen.

But what do you do when it's not up to you to make them happen? What if your child wants to go on a sleepover, but it's up to another parent to make that decision? What if she wants to join a sports team, but the choice is up to the coach? What if he wants a summer job, but that decision rests with the employer? Then, like Nehemiah, you can pray to God.

You may be tempted to not bother praying if your child's heart is set on something that seems very childish. But if you'd drive them across the city to a water slide to play with their friends because it's important to *them*, why wouldn't you also show your love by praying that this other desire be granted? It shouldn't be beneath you to pray about your child's heartfelt desires.

The Bible says, "The king's heart is in the hand of the LORD, like the rivers of water; He turns it wherever He wishes" (Proverbs 21:1 NKJV). So quote God's Word to Him today, reminding Him of His promises, and ask Him to move some "king's" heart to show your child favor.

Lord, I come before You with a simple request:
my child really has his/her heart set on something,
but it's not within my power to grant it. If it was up
to me, I'd certainly decide in their favor, because it
makes them happy and would be a good way for me
to show my love. Because it's important to my child,
it's important to me. So please give them favor in the
eyes of those who have the decision-making power,
Lord. In Jesus' name I pray. Amen.

FOR FURTHER THOUGHT

- Which activities, though unimportant to you, are very important to your child?

- How much effort do you put forth to make your child's desires come true?

- Why is it worth it to pray about "childish" activities and events?

49.

PRAYING FOR ENCOURAGEMENT

Nehemiah and the Jews were busy rebuilding Jerusalem's walls, but when Sanballat, a Horonite official, heard about it, he found it hilarious that they'd even try. After all, the stones of the former wall were buried under heaps of rubble, and many had been burned when Jerusalem was set ablaze and were now brittle and useless. Sanballat mocked, "What are these feeble Jews doing? . . . Can they revive the stones from the dusty rubble even the burned ones?" He called the Jews "feeble," thinking they didn't have the strength to dig out the huge stones and set them in place.

Tobiah, the Ammonite governor, agreed that they had no idea how to build a solid wall. He joked, "If a fox should jump on it, he would break their stone wall down!" (Nehemiah 4:2–3 NASB). They thought the Jews' efforts were laughable. When their comments were relayed to the Jews, many of them became discouraged. *Maybe*, they thought, *Sanballat and Tobiah are right.*

But when Nehemiah realized his men were becoming disheartened, he prayed, "Hear, O our God, how we are despised! Return their reproach on their own heads. . . . Do not forgive their iniquity and let not their sin be blotted out before You, for they have demoralized the builders" (vv. 4–5 NASB).

Nehemiah and his workers kept working and quickly became proficient at digging out the buried stones and hoisting them in place. Soon the whole wall around Jerusalem was built to half its height. As Nehemiah explained,

"The people had a mind to work" (v. 6 NASB).

When their enemies realized the Jews might actually succeed, they decided there was no way they could let that happen. So they tried to terrify them into stopping. They conspired to attack them, but Nehemiah set up sentries and he and his workers prayed continually. "We prayed to our God, and because of them we set up a guard against them day and night" (v. 9 NASB).

Worst of all, Jewish so-called prophets gave warnings "from God" that Nehemiah was doomed to fail. He wrote, "All of them were trying to frighten us, thinking, 'They will become discouraged with the work and it will not be done.' But now, O God, strengthen my hands." He also prayed, "Remember, O my God, Tobiah and Sanballat according to these works of theirs, and also. . .the prophets who were trying to frighten me" (6:9, 14 NASB).

Nehemiah prayed nonstop and continually spoke encouragement to his people, and God strengthened them so that in only fifty-two days the entire wall around Jerusalem was rebuilt. What a difference the inspiration and the power of God make!

Bullying, teasing, and harassment are common today. Perhaps your daughter is being picked on in school by cruel cliques who mock her appearance and put down everything she does. Maybe a neighborhood bully is calling your son a weakling and a sissy. This kind of mental cruelty can be devastating for children. Many bullies, like Sanballat and Tobiah, don't use actual physical violence but threaten to beat up smaller kids in order to terrorize them and make their lives miserable.

Not only should you talk to the proper authorities at your earliest opportunity, but you must pray. Even after the bullies have been warned by the school authorities or their parents, they may continue to threaten your child, give mocking looks, and whisper insults. They may even steal or deface your child's property. So be diligent to pray that they back off, become afraid to continue, or lose interest in tormenting your child.

Dear God, thank You for bringing this situation to my attention so I can help my child who is being bullied. Be with me as I contact the responsible adults who can resolve this situation. Help me to comfort my daughter and assure her that she's not ugly and worthless, like they're telling her. Help me to encourage my son and let him know he's not weak or stupid. I pray that my children will be open to my encouragement. In Jesus' name. Amen.

FOR FURTHER THOUGHT

- Why do bullies get such pleasure from picking on other kids?
- How did continual prayer help strengthen Nehemiah and his workers?
- Why is it important not only to take action but also to pray in such situations?

50.

PRAYING DESPITE WEAK FAITH

The priest Zacharias and his wife, Elizabeth, were very old. They had no children, and though Zacharias had prayed for a son for many years, he became increasingly discouraged and struggled to believe that God would answer. Then, when the situation looked utterly hopeless, the angel Gabriel appeared to him and said:

> *"Do not be afraid, Zacharias, for your prayer is heard; and your wife Elizabeth will bear you a son, and you shall call his name John. And you will have joy and gladness, and many will rejoice at his birth. For he will be great in the sight of the Lord. . . . He will also be filled with the Holy Spirit, even from his mother's womb. And he will turn many of the children of Israel to the Lord their God. He will also go before Him in the spirit and power of Elijah, 'to turn the hearts of the fathers to the children,' and the disobedient to the wisdom of the just, to make ready a people prepared for the Lord." (Luke 1:13–17 NKJV)*

To have an *ordinary* child at Zacharias's age was one thing. But to be asked to believe that his son would fulfill the prophecy about Elijah's coming (Malachi 4:5) confounded Zacharias's reason. He asked, "How shall I know this? For I am an old man, and my wife is well advanced in years" (Luke 1:18 NKJV). In other words, "This is amazing! Can you offer any proof that it will actually happen? After all, it's not even possible for us to have a baby at our age."

As punishment for his doubt, Zacharias became unable to speak until the angel's words were fulfilled. Then, after his son was born, Zacharias was filled with the Holy Spirit and prophesied, "You, child, will be called the prophet of the Highest; for you will go before the face of the Lord to prepare His ways, to give knowledge of salvation to His people by the remission of their sins" (vv. 76–77 NKJV).

Zacharias was like so many parents today—painfully aware of his need, driven to pray ceaselessly for a child, but not sure God would actually do such a miracle. And after he'd spent decades praying with no results, his faith was very weak. So when the angel made such amazing promises about his son, Zacharias doubted they could happen.

You may pray often for your children simply because the need is great and you have to cry out to God, but like Zacharias, you may not be certain He will actually grant your request.

The Bible cautions, "When you ask, you must believe and not doubt, because the one who doubts. . .should not expect to receive anything from the Lord" (James 1:6–7 NIV). But if God sees that you have a kernel of real faith, He can honor that. As one father said, "Lord, I believe; help my unbelief!" (Mark 9:24 NKJV). And Jesus did precisely that. Whatever criticism you may have of Zacharias, remember God's message of commendation to him: "Your prayer is heard." Since God answered, Zacharias must have had some genuine faith when he prayed.

Another possibility is that although Zacharias had prayed repeatedly during his younger years and through middle age, when he and his wife had finally become old, he thought the window of opportunity had passed, so his prayers tapered off. But God remembered his many petitions and answered years after he'd ceased praying. Sometimes God does a miracle despite your weak faith—made weak by a long period of testing—simply because He has great plans that can't be derailed.

Dear God, I've never identified with Zacharias before. I've seen him as a weak old man who lacked faith, and I've assumed that I wouldn't have doubted if an angel had appeared and given me that message. But I see how he stayed faithful to pray for years after it was "obvious" that no miracle would happen. Had I been in his situation, my faith might have weakened after such prolonged testing too. Help me to refuse to stop praying when things look impossible, even though my faith seems weak and tattered. In Jesus' name I pray. Amen.

FOR FURTHER THOUGHT

- Why would Zacharias keep on praying for a miracle if he had doubts?

- Do you think Zacharias still had a kernel of faith? Why or why not?

- Or do you think God answered his prayers years after he ceased hoping?

- Can you identify with Zacharias's struggle to believe God's promises for his son?

51.

A RICH FATHER'S FAITH

Job describes the privileged life the wealthy provide for their children: "They see their children established around them, their offspring before their eyes. Their homes are safe and free from fear. . . . They send forth their children as a flock; their little ones dance about. They sing to the music of timbrel and lyre; they make merry to the sound of the pipe. They spend their years in prosperity" (Job 21:8–9, 11–13 NIV).

James 2:5–6 (NKJV) says, "Has God not chosen the poor of this world to be rich in faith and heirs of the kingdom. . . ?" And of the poor James asks, "Do not the rich oppress you. . . ?" Many Christians, therefore, think that the wealthy have so much luxury that God shouldn't heal them on top of it. Let them go to the expensive specialists; healing should be reserved for the poor who have no other option.

There was once a well-to-do Jewish nobleman in Capernaum who couldn't buy health for his son when he was dying of a high fever. Now, when Jesus was at the Passover in Jerusalem, He did several miracles (John 2:23). Then He went to Cana in Galilee, and thousands of returning pilgrims spread the news of His miracles throughout Galilee. This nobleman heard about Jesus and hurried to Cana, eighteen miles away.

He arrived in town, found Jesus, and asked Him to come heal his son. He may have expected that because he was so important, Jesus would make the trip. At first, however, Jesus declined. To his credit, the nobleman didn't offer money to entice Him. Instead, he begged, "Sir, come down before my child dies!"

Jesus didn't wish to travel to Capernaum, so He said, "Go your way; your son lives." The nobleman could have insisted that Jesus needed to be present to heal. After all, wasn't that how it was done? Instead, he headed home. He didn't make it back that day and probably stopped at an inn. There were no cell phones, so he couldn't send a text message to get an update, but that night he went to sleep trusting in the Lord's healing.

The next morning he met his servants on the road, who told him that his son was cured. When the nobleman asked what time he'd recovered, they replied, "Yesterday at the seventh hour the fever left him." The nobleman realized that was the very time that Jesus had said, "Your son lives," so he and his entire household became believers (John 4:49–53 NKJV).

The Bible says, "Unto you that fear my name shall the Sun of righteousness arise with healing in his wings" (Malachi 4:2 KJV). God doesn't differentiate between the children of the rich and the poor. All can come to Him. The problem, however, is usually with their parents. The rich frequently trust that their money can solve all their problems and consequently don't pray when their kids are sick or in trouble. This is why the Bible says, "Command those who are rich. . .not to be haughty, nor to trust in uncertain riches but in the living God" (1 Timothy 6:17 NKJV).

Riches aren't evil in themselves. After all, the Bible says, "May the LORD cause you to flourish, both you and your children" (Psalm 115:14 NIV). But whatever the size of your bank account, you should come to Jesus as a mother for your children. The nobleman didn't pray a long prayer. He first explained his son's desperate need to Jesus and then made a short emotional request. But he had faith, so it was enough. James asks, "Has God not chosen the poor of this world to be rich in faith. . . ?" (James 2:5 NKJV). Yes, He has. But the wealthy can be rich in faith too—if they trust in God, not money.

Dear God, my money and my health plan can get me some of the best doctors and medical care in the world, but there are times when all my resources are useless in the face of serious illness. So I humble myself and turn to You, the great Healer. I ask You to do what the doctors are unable to do. Spare my child, Lord. He/she is Your child. I place him/her in Your hands and ask You to do the miracle that only You can do. In Jesus' name I ask. Amen.

FOR FURTHER THOUGHT

- Do the very wealthy have a right to God's healing? Why or why not?
- Why do the rich often not pray when trouble hits?
- Why does the Lord's initial answer sometimes sound like a "no" to us?
- Why does God often not answer prayer the way we expect Him to?

52.

THE LORD'S PRAYER

When Jesus' disciples requested, "Lord, teach us to pray" (Luke 11:1 NKJV), Jesus replied by teaching them the Lord's Prayer. The versions in Matthew and Luke are slightly different, so we'll quote the one from Matthew, since it's the most familiar. It reads, "Our Father in heaven, hallowed be Your name. Your kingdom come. Your will be done on earth as it is in heaven. Give us this day our daily bread. And forgive us our debts, as we forgive our debtors. And do not lead us into temptation, but deliver us from the evil one. For Yours is the kingdom and the power and the glory forever. Amen" (Matthew 6:9–13 NKJV).

The Lord's Prayer is a model of simplicity and covers all the bases. Not only is this prayer beautiful, but its brevity makes a powerful point: state your requests simply and clearly.

Now, because Jesus said, "When you pray, say" (Luke 11:2 NKJV)—then supplied the precise words—many people think this is *exactly* what He intended Christians to pray. So they recite the prayer word for word, sometimes several times in a row. But this prayer is not meant as a magical mantra. Christians should think about what it's saying while they're praying it. If your children are memorizing Bible verses, make sure the Lord's Prayer is among them. And while they're committing it to memory, teach them what it means. Here are some thoughts you can share:

"Our Father in heaven. . ." The opening words remind

your children that God is their all-powerful Father, and this means He loves them and is good to them. Jesus told some parents, "If you. . .know how to give good gifts to your children, how much more will your Father in heaven give good gifts to those who ask him!" (Matthew 7:11 NIV).

"Hallowed be Your name." These words remind your children to worship God and keep His name hallowed, or holy, because God Himself is holy. Therefore, they shouldn't say His name lightly (Exodus 20:7).

"Your kingdom come." Paul tells us, "The kingdom of God is. . .righteousness and peace and joy in the Holy Spirit" (Romans 14:17 NKJV). Your children should desire these virtues in their lives here and now.

"Your will be done on earth as it is in heaven." When your children pray this, they aren't just praying for peace on earth; they're also agreeing that they'll yield to God's will for their *own* lives.

"Give us this day our daily bread." Your children can trust God to supply what they need day by day because the Bible promises, "My God will meet all your needs" (Philippians 4:19 NIV).

"Forgive us our debts, as we forgive our debtors." This sentence reminds your children that they continually need to be forgiven. "If we confess our sins, He is faithful and just to forgive us our sins and to cleanse us from all unrighteousness" (1 John 1:9 NKJV). Your children also should daily forgive others who have offended them.

"Do not lead us into temptation, but deliver us from the evil one." God can help your children resist temptation and can protect them from the devil. "The Lord is faithful, and he will strengthen you and protect you from the evil one" (2 Thessalonians 3:3 NIV).

"For Yours is the kingdom and the power and the glory forever." Your children will live forever in God's glorious heavenly kingdom, so they should think about it and focus on it even now.

"Amen." This means "Let it be so!"

> *Father in heaven, help my children to treat Your*
> *name as holy. Help them to value the righteousness,*
> *peace, and joy of Your kingdom. Help them to yield*
> *to Your will on earth now, just as those in heaven do.*
> *Please supply their daily bread and all their other*
> *needs. In Your love and mercy, forgive my children's*
> *sins, and help them to forgive those who sin against*
> *them. Lord, give them strength to resist temptation,*
> *and protect them from attacks of the evil one. Help*
> *them every day to remember that they'll live forever in*
> *Your glorious kingdom. In Jesus' name I pray. Amen.*

FOR FURTHER THOUGHT

- Have you helped your children memorize the Lord's Prayer?
- When and how will you share with them what this prayer means?
- How does God's role as their Father ensure that He will be good to them?

53.

SEVERELY TESTED FAITH

One of the most difficult positions a mother can find herself in is to watch her child suffer from serious illness or injury and not be able to do anything to help.

One day when Jesus was in Capernaum, a huge crowd gathered around Him. Suddenly a man named Jairus, a ruler of the synagogue, burst through the throng. He bowed at Jesus' feet and begged, "My little daughter lies at the point of death. Come and lay Your hands on her, that she may be healed, and she will live" (Mark 5:23 NKJV).

What the Bible doesn't describe is that—just like today—Jairus and his wife most likely had called a doctor when their daughter became ill. Physicians back then didn't know as much as those today, but they had practical skills and a good grasp of natural medicines and treatments. But this case was beyond their ability. At that point, all the parents could do was pray.

When he heard that Jesus was in Capernaum, Jairus rushed to where He was and begged Him to heal his daughter. So Jesus went with him, and the multitude followed. Then a woman suffering from bleeding came up behind Jesus and touched His garment, and He immediately stopped. The crowd stopped too, though Jairus seems to have continued walking. When Jesus learned who had touched Him and why, He assured the woman that she'd been healed.

While He was still speaking, however, messengers came from Jairus's house and told him, "Your daughter is dead.

Why trouble the Teacher any further?" (Mark 5:35 NKJV).

Jairus rushed back to Jesus and said, "My daughter has just died, but come and lay Your hand on her and she will live" (Matthew 9:18 NKJV). Jairus still believed, but his faith was being severely tested, so Jesus said, "Do not be afraid; only believe."

When He came to the house, He saw a tumult and women weeping loudly. Jesus shooed everyone out and entered the room where the young girl lay. Only Peter, James, John, and the girl's parents accompanied Him. Then Jesus took the child by the hand and said, "Little girl, I say to you, arise" (Mark 5:36–41 NKJV). Immediately she arose from her deathbed. Everyone was stunned, and the news of this miracle swept across that entire region.

Jairus petitioned Jesus *twice*—first when his daughter was dying and barely alive, and again after she had just died. He expressed faith in both prayers and never stopped believing that Jesus could restore his daughter. And Jesus did the miracle!

Note, however, that although God *can* raise the dead, He doesn't often do so. Jesus Himself, during His three and a half years of ministry, raised only three people from death. And even Christians who insist that Jesus' command to raise the dead (Matthew 10:8) applies to believers today must admit that this happens only on rare occasions. It's not something you can expect every day.

Nevertheless, this biblical account offers several practical lessons you can learn and apply to your prayers for your children. Many parents pray and trust God to act in difficult situations, but their faith fails when bad news comes and things suddenly look impossible. The messengers asked, "Why trouble the Teacher any further?" Some people think that when things get desperate, to *continue* praying is just to bother God for no reason. But not only can God do the difficult—He can do the impossible.

The Bible says, "The righteous will never be shaken. . . .They will have no fear of bad news; their hearts are steadfast, trusting in the LORD" (Psalm 112:6–7 NIV). So believe God for miracles. He has the power to do them.

> *Dear God, I thank You that You're powerful enough to literally raise the dead. Though You don't do it often, the fact that You do it at all is proof of Your great power and encourages me that You're more than able to answer my everyday prayers and do miracles in my life. I pray that You'll do miracles in my children's lives also. I'm thankful for Your intervention even if those miracles take a little time. In the name of Your Son, Jesus, I pray. Amen.*

FOR FURTHER THOUGHT

- What difficult situation in your child's life are you praying for right now?
- Has God ever come through for you in a difficult or "impossible" situation?
- Have you ever been shaken by bad news but trusted God anyway?

54.

THE PROOF IS IN THE FRUIT

One time a large crowd followed and pressed around Jesus, at times almost crushing Him. In this crowd was a woman who had experienced constant bleeding for twelve years. She had suffered ineffective treatments from many doctors and had spent every bit of money she had, yet nothing had healed her.

The woman's bloody discharge made her ceremonially impure, and anyone who touched her also became "unclean" (Leviticus 15:25–33), so she couldn't ask Jesus to lay His hands on her and pray for her. She wasn't allowed to touch anyone either, so she decided just to brush her fingers against the edge of His clothing—so lightly that Jesus wouldn't even feel it. As a precaution, she sneaked up behind Him where He couldn't see her. She thought, "If I just touch his clothes, I will be healed" (Mark 5:28 NIV). That was her unspoken prayer.

She was like so many poor people in third world countries who can't afford to pay for electricity and decide to hook up an illegal connection, tap into the city line, and siphon off power. The main difference, however, was that her faith was real, so her tap—though unorthodox—was legitimate. And her faith was mightily rewarded.

The instant she touched the fringe of Jesus' cloak, her bleeding stopped and she felt that she was healed. Jesus knew in that same instant that a surge of power had left Him, so He turned and asked, "Who touched my clothes?" His disciples were baffled that He would ask such a question, and said, "You see the people crowding against you, and yet you can ask, 'Who touched me?' " (vv. 30–31 NIV).

But Jesus kept looking around to see who had done it. He insisted, "Someone touched me; I know that power has gone out from me." Then the woman, realizing she would soon be found out, came forward, fell at His feet, and, trembling with fear, confessed the whole truth. Jesus said to her, "Daughter, your faith has healed you. Go in peace" (Luke 8:46, 48 NIV).

This woman had genuine faith, and when she made contact with Jesus, healing power flowed out of Him and into her body. Children today also need to touch Jesus, to make contact with Him. They need to connect with God if they're to have His life coursing through them.

Jesus said, "I am the vine; you are the branches. If you remain in me and I in you, you will bear much fruit; apart from me you can do nothing." He also said, "Remain in me, as I also remain in you. No branch can bear fruit by itself; it must remain in the vine. Neither can you bear fruit unless you remain in me" (John 15:4–5 NIV). A branch must be firmly connected to the grapevine if it is to have the life-giving sap flowing through it.

It may seem sometimes that your children have made only light contact, but if their faith is real, the evidence will begin to appear in their lives. Jesus said, "Every good tree bears good fruit, but a bad tree bears bad fruit. A good tree cannot bear bad fruit, nor can a bad tree bear good fruit. . . . Therefore by their fruits you will know them" (Matthew 7:17–18, 20 NKJV).

Of course, you shouldn't expect your children to become perfect overnight, any more than you yourself would like to try to live up to such expectations. But changes should begin to appear. And as a parent, you nurture this growth by modeling a godly example for your children, by reading God's Word with them, and by praying with them and for them.

Father, thank You that You ordained that "whoever calls on the name of the Lord shall be saved" (Acts 2:21 NKJV). Thank You that I can help Your Spirit's presence grow in my children's lives by praying for them. So help me to be faithful to pray. Jesus, may Your Spirit take vigorous root in their hearts and be continually watered by prayer, nourished by Your Word, and sheltered from destructive storms. May You bear abundant fruit in their lives! In Jesus' name. Amen.

FOR FURTHER THOUGHT

- Why is it so important that your children truly touch God?

- What part do their simple, faith-filled prayers have in this process?

- How do your prayers nurture your children's growth in Christ?

- Is good fruit something you can produce yourself?

55.

A Prayer for Salvation

Jesus did a huge miracle by multiplying a few loaves and fishes into enough food to feed five thousand men, as well as many women and children. The crowd, eager for a Messiah who would continually do food miracles for them, wanted to make Jesus king immediately (John 6:14–15), but He knew their selfish motives and crossed the Sea of Galilee to get away from them. Several men, however, followed Him.

Jesus said, "You seek Me, not because you saw signs, but because you ate of the loaves and were filled. Do not work for the food which perishes, but for the food which endures to eternal life." Upon hearing this, they asked Him, "What shall we do, so that we may work the works of God?" Jesus answered, "This is the work of God, that you believe in Him whom He has sent."

But they asked, "What then do You do for a sign, so that we may see, and believe You?" They then hinted which sign they wanted most: "Our fathers ate the manna in the wilderness; as it is written, 'He gave them bread out of heaven to eat.'" Jesus answered, "It is My Father who gives you the true bread out of heaven. For the bread of God is that which comes down out of heaven, and gives life to the world." So they implored, "Lord, always give us this bread." Jesus replied, "I am the bread of life" (John 6:26–35 NASB).

Millions of people today pray, "What shall we do, so that we may work the works of God?" They're desperate to know exactly what good things they need to do to earn eternal life, to be allowed to enter heaven. But the only "work" they must do is to believe in Jesus, to partake of the Bread of Life.

The most important prayer you can pray as a mother is for your children to be saved, to truly know God and have His spiritual life within them. Without this, all else in their lives is dead and empty. God longs for your children to hunger after Him and to invite Him in with believing prayer so that He can then pour His life into their spirits. "Because you are his sons, God sent the Spirit of his Son into our hearts" (Galatians 4:6 NIV).

It's not enough for your children to believe that Jesus exists, just as it's not enough for them to believe that a piece of bread exists. It's not even enough for them to bite into it and chew it. They must swallow it and it must become part of their being for it to do them any good. Just so, they not only must believe in Jesus but must receive Him into their hearts to be saved. "As many as received him, to them gave he power to become the sons of God, even to them that believe on his name" (John 1:12 KJV).

God longs for the Spirit of His Son not just to enter their hearts but to take solid root and grow steadily. Paul compared this progression to pregnancy and delivery. He wrote, "My little children, for whom I labor in birth. . . until Christ is formed in you" (Galatians 4:19 NKJV). It's not God's plan for new life to begin and then to be ignored or abandoned; for your children to grow into the mature individuals God wants them to be, Christ must take solid root and His presence must grow in their lives.

These are the most important things you should pray for in your children's lives. Look for opportunities to present the Gospel in all its simplicity to them, and lead them in a sincere prayer to invite Jesus into their lives.

Dear Father in heaven, I pray that You will cause a spiritual hunger to grow in my children's hearts so that they'll be hungry for Your Spirit and the eternal life only You can give them. May they truly know that they're saved not by their good works but by a simple faith in Your Son, Jesus Christ. May they receive the Spirit of Your Son into their hearts. In Jesus' name I pray. Amen.

FOR FURTHER THOUGHT

- Why isn't it enough to believe that a piece of bread exists and is nourishing?
- How can Christ's Spirit take firm root and grow in your child's heart?
- Have your children invited Christ into their lives?

56.

STRONG AND STEADY FAITH

One day Jesus told His disciples to get into a boat and cross the lake while He stayed and sent the crowds away. When darkness came, the boat was a long distance from land, battered by waves and fighting headwinds. About three o'clock in the morning, Jesus came to them across the surging sea. When the disciples saw Him walking on the waves, they shouted, "It is a ghost!" But Jesus said, "Take courage, it is I; do not be afraid."

Peter blurted out, "Lord, if it is You, command me to come to You on the water." Jesus replied, "Come!" So Peter got out of the boat and strode on the heaving waters toward Him. Some way out, however, he became frightened by the wind and waves and began to sink. He cried, "Lord, save me!" so Jesus grabbed him and kept him on the surface. Then He asked, "You of little faith, why did you doubt?" (Matthew 14:26–31 NASB).

Peter had been filled with a sudden surge of faith and stepped out on the water. Great faith for unusual acts often comes suddenly—but can be just as suddenly lost, as Peter learned. "We walk by faith, not by sight" (2 Corinthians 5:7 NKJV). Fear and doubt short-circuited his faith, and he could no longer do the miraculous.

Jesus asked, "Why did you doubt?" Can we actually choose to have faith or *not* have it? Yes, people do this all the time. They believe for miracles in fair weather but lose their confidence when trouble hits. This is especially true of children. They don't have the years of life experience that you do to know that even though things may look dark at present, God will eventually come through.

Small children often exhibit boundless energy. While the adults are sitting on park benches talking, their kids are running around everywhere, shouting and laughing. But later on, the kids are zonked out while the adults are still laughing. It's the same with older kids: they may have the energy to set a brisk pace when hiking, but after several miles they're ready to rest, while the adults—if they're in shape—are still going.

Adults may not have flash-in-the-pan energy but generally have more stamina. It's the same with faith. Many people "hear the message and immediately receive it with joy. But since they don't have deep roots, they don't last long" (Matthew 13:20–21 NLT). And here is where this applies to you and your children: Children often have childlike faith. No surprises there. They believe God readily and sometimes get miraculous answers to prayer as a result. But often you must fight a sustained battle to get your answers. This is where stamina comes in, as you patiently stand your ground and refuse to give up, even when the heavens seem like bronze overhead (Deuteronomy 28:23) and God's ears seem shut.

When your children are sick or waiting impatiently for God to respond, you as their mother must stand firm, resisting the battering of life's storms. "We are no longer to be children, tossed here and there by waves and carried about by every wind of doctrine" (Ephesians 4:14 NASB). Children's faith is often easily moved, so they need a strong hand to hold them steady. You can provide this. When they begin to sink in the storm like Peter did, you must reach out, take their hand, and keep them from going under.

Children may vacillate a lot and be easily misled, and you may wonder at times how they're going to make it. The answer is: God intends that you be there to protect and guide them. And this includes praying for them. A Christian proverb says, "God tempers the wind to the shorn lambs." May you, like God, shield your children from life's harshest blows while they're young and tender.

Father in heaven, help me to be a steady, grounding influence and to continually encourage my children to believe that You won't fail them, no matter how dark and hopeless things may appear. Help me to guide my children in Your ways. Make them rooted and grounded in the truth so they're not battered and broken by the winds and waves of life. Help me to encourage their faith by calmly and patiently standing my ground. In Jesus' name. Amen.

FOR FURTHER THOUGHT

- Why do children often have great faith but also give up easily?

- Why do adults generally have more stamina, including in spiritual matters?

- How is false doctrine in Ephesians 4:14 like wind and waves?

57.

An Unworthy Parent's Prayer

At one point, Jesus and His twelve disciples left Israel and traveled north to Phoenicia. A large Jewish population lived there, and it was to one of these expatriates that Jesus went. He didn't announce His arrival, and He didn't intend to launch a public ministry there. "He entered a house and wanted no one to know it" (Mark 7:24 NKJV).

The house was spacious enough to accommodate Jesus and His twelve disciples, so it probably belonged to a wealthy Jewish merchant. It was outside the cities in "the *region* of Tyre and Sidon" (v. 24 NKJV, emphasis added). Like most such homes of the time, it would've been surrounded by a shady garden and an outer wall. This affluent Jew must have been delighted to host a famous rabbi from Israel. But someone was about to crash his private party, because Jesus "could not be hidden" (v. 24 NKJV).

The Bible doesn't explain how a local Phoenician woman made it through the gate and into his house. Nor does it explain why the homeowner didn't immediately escort her out. Possibly she was one of his wealthy neighbors. That would explain why *she* knew Jesus was there, but the rest of the city didn't. (Otherwise, there would have been a huge crowd at the door. See Mark 2:1–2.)

Now, the Phoenicians were Gentiles, and the Jews didn't invite Gentiles into their homes (Acts 10:28). But hearing that a wonderful Jewish healer was there, the woman barged into the house crying, "Lord, Son of David, have mercy on me! My daughter is demon-possessed and suffering terribly." Son of David was a title that meant "Messiah." Now, where had she heard *that*? From her Jewish neighbor, no doubt.

Jesus didn't answer her, and it appears from His comments that they were gathered around the table, eating. But she kept crying out. Talk about ignoring all social decorum. Soon Jesus' disciples urged Him, "Send her away, for she keeps crying out after us." Jesus turned to the woman and said, "I was sent only to the lost sheep of Israel." Desperate, she knelt before Him, insisting, "Lord, help me!" (Matthew 15:22–25 NIV).

Jesus replied, "First let the children eat all they want . . .for it is not right to take the children's bread and toss it to the dogs" (Mark 7:27 NIV). She replied, "Yes it is, Lord. Even the dogs eat the crumbs that fall from their master's table." Jesus said, "Woman, you have great faith! Your request is granted." And when she returned to her home, she found her daughter healed (Matthew 15:27–28 NIV).

This woman had broken nearly a dozen rules of polite society rushing in to petition Jesus, and for a while, it looked as if she might not get what she wanted. But she wouldn't be put off, and her great faith ensured that her prayer was answered. Her dogged persistence also helped get an answer. She knew that Jesus could help her daughter, and since He was her *only* hope, she refused to take no for an answer.

Now, God had sent Jesus to the Jews. After they'd all heard the message, it could go to the Gentiles. . .but not before. This was why Jesus first ignored the woman and said, "First let the children eat." But her faith and persistence bumped her forward in line and enabled her daughter to get the help she needed.

Many times, Jesus answers the prayers of unworthy

people. They come to Him with all their faults, problems, and rough manners, brokenhearted over their children, and He does a miracle. They break all our nice Christian rules—even while praying—but God looks past that to their faith. And He will do the same for you. So even if *you* feel unworthy, cast yourself on His mercy and implore Him to help your children.

Dear Jesus, if I had been there that day, I probably would've been like one of Your disciples and said, "Send her away." But how many times do I myself come before You like a beggar without proper manners, utterly unworthy to have You hear my prayer or answer it? Yet help me not to look upon my own shortcomings and failures, but let me come boldly before You, like the Phoenician woman did, that I may obtain mercy for my children. In Your name I pray. Amen.

FOR FURTHER THOUGHT

- Why does God often answer the prayers of people who break so many rules?
- Why did Jesus heal the daughter of an "unworthy Gentile"?
- An old hymn speaks of "Jesus, friend of sinners." Is this phrase true?

58.

PRAYING FOR ANNOYING CHILDREN

Paul wrote to the believers in Philippi, "I thank my God upon every remembrance of you, always in every prayer of mine making request for you all with joy" (Philippians 1:3–4 NKJV). Does this sound like something you would say about *your* children? Do you give thanks to God each time you think about them? Every time you pray for them, do you do so with joy? Probably not *every* time. And if some of your children are going through a phase where they're squabbling, talking back, or whining, you no doubt feel heavyhearted, not joyful.

Researchers have discovered that the sound of a crying baby elicits different responses from men and women. Women generally feel sympathy and an instinct to calm the infant. Men usually feel annoyed. But both fathers and mothers can become exasperated by constant misbehavior—mothers because they often have to deal with it all day long, and fathers because they're expected to deal with it the moment they arrive home from work.

If you're very honest, perhaps you have a child whose habit of whining even causes you to dislike that child. Maybe it's not just their tone of voice that causes resentment. Their rebellious attitude or willful manner gets to you—and firm discipline only slowly seems to be making a dent. If so, you may find yourself becoming frustrated easily and not know what to do.

Well, you definitely should pray for your child. At the same time, you need to be careful not to despise them.

Jesus said, "Take heed that you do not despise one of these little ones, for I say to you that in heaven their angels always see the face of My Father who is in heaven" (Matthew 18:10 NKJV). You may think, *Surely Jesus was just describing good, obedient, happy children.* But do you suppose that the angels of whiny or misbehaving children *don't* see the face of the Father?

Maybe something else that grates on you is how two of your children are always fighting. They never seem to get along, and you feel like calling them "the sons of thunder" (Mark 3:17 KJV). If they're not actually hitting each other, one is constantly teasing and reducing the other to tears. This is nothing new. "Sarah saw Ishmael. . .making fun of her son, Isaac" (Genesis 21:9 NLT). Or consider the prophet Elisha: "There came forth little children out of the city, and mocked him" (2 Kings 2:23 KJV).

The fact is, children can be mean, and for a prolonged period, life with your kids may be an ongoing drama of quarrels, crying, and misbehavior, interspersed with happy times. But through it all, God expects you to pray for your children—in love. One day, James and John ("the sons of thunder") asked Jesus, "Lord, do You want us to command fire to come down from heaven and consume them, just as Elijah did?" But Jesus answered, "You do not know what manner of spirit you are of" (Luke 9:54–55 NKJV).

While you must pray seriously about your children's behavior—likely they don't give you constant joy like the Philippians did Paul—you also should watch what spirit you're walking in. Be sure you're motivated by love, not frustration. It's only natural to be upset by disobedience, but consistent discipline and faithful prayer are the answer, not anger. If you keep a steady attitude and determine to discipline in love, the day will come when even trying children give you joy.

Dear God, I've had just about all the bad behavior I can stand for one day. Please, Lord, give me patience. Help me to correct and discipline my children in love, not in anger. Help me not to give up on them, Lord, just as You don't give up on them—or on me. Although sometimes You seem to be moving extremely slowly in transforming my children, with barely any change evident day after day, I trust that You hear my prayers and are at work. In Jesus' name I pray. Amen.

FOR FURTHER THOUGHT

- How can you avoid losing your temper when your children misbehave?
- What kinds of prayers do you pray when your kids get under your skin?
- How can you ensure that you're disciplining in the right spirit?

59.

BLESSING YOUNG CHILDREN

Many of Jesus' prayers aren't recorded, which is understandable considering how often He prayed. But surprisingly, this is true of even His best-known, most beloved prayers. We're talking, of course, about the time when Jesus blessed the children. We don't know whether He simply prayed a couple of sentences over each child or whether He prayed longer prayers—but one thing we do know: after the Master blessed them, they had a special touch of God on their lives from that day forward.

"One day some parents brought their children to Jesus so he could lay his hands on them and pray for them. But the disciples scolded the parents for bothering him. But Jesus said, 'Let the children come to me. Don't stop them! For the kingdom of heaven belongs to those who are like these children.' And he placed his hands on their heads and blessed them before he left" (Matthew 19:13–15 NLT).

Mark's Gospel adds this detail: "And he took the children in his arms, placed his hands on them and blessed them" (Mark 10:16 NIV). Artists often show Jesus seated with one or two toddlers on His lap, with a few more older children leaning against His knees, their mothers looking on in the background. It's a beautiful picture, but it's not entirely accurate.

Mark also tells us, "He took the children in his arms, placed his hands on them and blessed them." Jesus wasn't necessarily sitting and holding several toddlers on His lap at once. He very likely was standing, held several children one at a time in His arms, and prayed over them individually.

According to Luke's Gospel, the children were "babes," toddlers and probably even babies in diapers. Jesus' disciples considered the parents' desire to have Jesus bless such young children to be an interruption of more important adult business. Jesus had just spent hours ministering to people, and He was tired and wrapping things up so He could move on to the next place. The last thing He needed, they figured, was to indulge some parents' petty requests.

Yet, as Jesus pointed out, His disciples shouldn't have forbidden the parents to bring their little children to Him for blessing, because God's kingdom is made up of those who have just such childlike faith. You can be sure that after this incident the disciples considered blessing young children to be a legitimate part of Jesus' ministry.

An important point here is that Jesus views the simple faith of children to be both authentic and sufficient. The fact that they lack understanding of doctrinal matters isn't an obstacle to their entering the kingdom of heaven. In fact, adults require this same uncomplicated faith if they're to be saved.

The fact that Jesus gave such priority to blessing children should encourage you to do the same. Never neglect to pray for your small ones. Just because they can't understand the details of serving God doesn't mean they're not worth praying for. You can pray that sincere faith will be born in their hearts and that they will continue to believe in and love God as they grow older. You can pray that God will fulfill His will in their lives. And you can pray that He will put His angels around them to protect them as they go through their days.

Father, I thank You for this important lesson.
Help me never to underestimate how important
young children are to You. They have genuine,
powerful faith, faith we all should seek to emulate.
Help me to remember to bring my little ones to
You in prayer, asking You to bless and protect them
and to prepare their hearts for a life of service to You.
May I never think that I needn't bother praying
or them. In Jesus' name I ask. Amen.

FOR FURTHER THOUGHT

- How important is it to pray for God to bless very young children?

- Does Jesus accept children's simple faith? Is it sufficient to save them?

- Why must all adults have the simple faith of young children?

60.

PRAY AND NEVER GIVE UP

You may happen to have a very determined child who simply won't stop pestering you when they want something. While continual whining may earn them a time-out rather than what they're seeking, the fact is, insistent adults who refuse to take no for an answer have a good chance of getting what they want. Assertiveness coaches sometimes tell people to use a "broken record" approach—keep insisting on the exact same thing, over and over again, without any letup.

One day Jesus told His disciples some amazing secrets of how to pray. Like most people, they became perplexed and discouraged when God seemed to ignore their oft-repeated prayers. So Jesus told a parable to show that they should pray and keep on praying and never give up.

"There was a judge in a certain city," He said, "who neither feared God nor cared about people. A widow of that city came to him repeatedly, saying, 'Give me justice in this dispute with my enemy.' The judge ignored her for a while, but finally he said to himself, 'I don't fear God or care about people, but this woman is driving me crazy. I'm going to see that she gets justice, because she is wearing me out with her constant requests!' "

Then Jesus said, "Learn a lesson from this unjust judge. Even he rendered a just decision in the end. So don't you think God will surely give justice to his chosen people who cry out to him day and night? Will he keep putting them off? I tell you, he will grant justice to them quickly!

But when the Son of Man returns, how many will he find on the earth who have faith?" (Luke 18:1–8 NLT).

Some people think Jesus was saying that God is just like the unjust judge—unwilling to answer the pitiful pleas of desperate people until they pester Him to death. But that misses the plain point of His parable. Jesus was saying that if even an unjust judge could finally be moved to act, how much more will your loving and just heavenly Father?

This point is brought out by Jesus' statement to a crowd: "If you then, being evil, know how to give good gifts to your children, how much more will your Father who is in heaven give good things to those who ask Him!" (Matthew 7:11 NKJV). Indeed—much more!

You may be crying out for your children but feel like God is putting you off or turning a deaf ear to you. But continue crying out. He loves your children very much, and He hears you. So "pray and never give up" (Luke 18:1 NLT). There will be times—perhaps quite a few times—when you'll need to pray for the same thing for your children again and again. So don't get discouraged. Be persistent.

You may feel like throwing up your hands and asking, "Why can't I just pray for something once and be done with it?" Well, you can try that if you want to, but the fact remains: God doesn't always answer prayer immediately but frequently requires you to persist and not give up. That is, in fact, the entire point of Jesus' parable.

An answer may be slow in coming for several reasons: (1) God may be testing you to reveal what's in your heart (Deuteronomy 8:2–5); (2) the devil may be fighting to prevent you from receiving an answer (Daniel 10:1–13; 1 Thessalonians 2:18); or (3) it's not the right time for the answer yet (Acts 10:1–4; Revelation 6:9–11).

Regardless of whether you understand all the reasons God may require you to come before Him continually, your children's well-being and future may depend upon your doing so.

Lord God, help me to persevere for my children's needs. I confess that it's difficult to keep praying, day after day, and not receive an answer. I'm often tempted to think that what I'm asking for must not be Your will, or that You don't love me and my children. But I know that some things that take a while definitely are Your will! And I know You do love my children. So help me to continue holding on, praying without giving up, and fighting my way through to the finish. In Jesus' name I pray. Amen.

FOR FURTHER THOUGHT

- Why do persistent people frequently get what they insist upon?

- Why do you think some of your answers to prayer have been delayed?

- Do you sometimes understand the reason for a delay but still don't *like* it?

61.

SHAMELESS PERSISTENCE IN PRAYER

You'll always be a mother to your children, even years after they leave home. Whether you barely prayed for them or upheld them in prayer every day, whether they're fully ready or not, the time comes when they must make their own way in the world.

Most adult children are eager to be on their way, but some are set adrift in society simply because their parents can no longer care for them. Such was the case with Bartimaeus. His name meant "Son of Timaeus," so he bore eternal testimony to who his father was—and in this case, his father hadn't been able to care for him. Bartimaeus had been born blind, so when it came time for him to go out on his own, he was forced to humble himself day after day by begging for spare change.

Jesus encountered Bartimaeus in Jericho. As He and His disciples were leaving the city, a large crowd followed Him. Bartimaeus was sitting beside the road, just outside the gates. With him was another blind beggar.

When Bartimaeus heard who was passing by, he began to shout, "Jesus, Son of David, have mercy on me!" Several people scolded him, saying, "Be quiet!" but he only shouted louder, "Son of David, have mercy on me!" Jesus finally heard him and said, "Tell him to come here." So the crowd told him, "Come on, he's calling you!" Bartimaeus threw aside his ragged coat and bowl of coins and came to Jesus. The other blind man followed.

"What do you want me to do for you?" Jesus asked.

"My Rabbi," Bartimaeus said, "I want to see!" The other blind man echoed his plea. Jesus touched their eyes and said, "Go, for your faith has healed you." Instantly both men could see (Mark 10:47–52 NLT; see also Matthew 20:29–34).

This is a powerful lesson in persistence. With so many people ordering them to be quiet and not make a fuss, the blind men easily could have given up. But they persisted, calling out again and again, getting ever louder.

Jesus once told a parable about a man whose friend arrived at midnight, but he had nothing to serve him. He banged on a friend's door, woke him up, and asked to borrow some bread. The man insisted he couldn't get up to help, but Jesus said, "I tell you this. . .if you keep knocking long enough, he will get up and give you whatever you need because of your shameless persistence. And so I tell you, keep on asking, and you will receive what you ask for" (Luke 11:8–9 NLT).

The two blind men had "shameless persistence." Every day they were forced to make a public spectacle of themselves by begging, so this was nothing new. They now created a real scene and refused to be shamed into shutting up. The crowd thought Jesus heard the beggars but was ignoring them, and so the crowd wanted them to politely accept His decision. In reality, Jesus *didn't* hear them over the noise of the crowd until they raised a real ruckus.

As a mother, you need to teach your children important life skills so they know how to manage a bank account, drive a car, and do an honest day's work. But you also need to teach them how to pray, because there will be many, many times in their lives when only God can help them, and they'll need to know how to claim His Word, petition

Him persistently, and receive what they need.

One of the best ways to teach your children how to pray is to pray with them so they can learn from watching and hearing you. This comes naturally when they're little, since most Christian parents pray with their children when they tuck them in at night. But they can also witness you praying when they're older, during family devotions at dinner or during any emergency or time of need.

Father in heaven, thank You that You'll never abandon me. You promised, "I will never leave you nor forsake you" (Hebrews 13:5 NKJV). I thank You also that my children will always be able to depend on You, even when they're out of my care. I want them to be confident and self-sufficient, Lord, but help them also to have the shameless persistence of a humble beggar so that they can receive what they need from You. In Jesus' name I pray. Amen.

FOR FURTHER THOUGHT

- Do you have "shameless persistence" when you pray? If not, why not?
- How can concern about people's opinions get in the way of prayer being answered?
- Why does it help to have a beggar's attitude when praying to God?

62.

YIELDING TO GOD'S WILL

When Jesus went to the Garden of Gethsemane, on the flank of the Mount of Olives, He left His disciples in the lower garden while He went higher up. He took Peter, James, and John with Him, saying, "Stay here and keep watch with me." Then, going a little farther, He prayed desperately, "My Father, if it is possible, may this cup be taken from me. Yet not as I will, but as you will." Later, He returned and found His disciples sleeping. He went away a second time and prayed, "My Father, if it is not possible for this cup to be taken away unless I drink it, may your will be done."

When Jesus returned, He found the three men sleeping again. So he left them and prayed a third time, saying the same words (Matthew 26:38–39, 42–44 NIV). And being in anguish, He prayed so intensely that His sweat was like great drops of blood falling to the ground (Luke 22:42–44).

The main lesson here is Jesus' complete yieldedness to His Father's will, however painful it was. He had said previously, "I do not seek My own will but the will of the Father who sent Me" (John 5:30 NKJV). Sometimes you too will be asked to make painful sacrifices, and though you could get out of them if you really wanted to, God will bless you for yielding to Him.

When it comes to your children, they're not likely to be asked to make painful sacrifices. . .although it might seem to them like they are. Nevertheless, the principle is the same. Children too must learn to say, "Not as I will, but as you will." Especially when your kids are young, yieldedness may be understood in light of God's commandment: "Honor your father and your mother" (Exodus 20:12 NIV). And what does it mean to *honor* them?

Paul gives the New Testament version of this commandment, saying, "Children, obey your parents in everything, for this pleases the Lord" (Colossians 3:20 NIV). If children are to obey their parents in *everything*, they'll have to submit their wills *often* and say, "Your will be done."

If God has blessed you with docile kids, obedient and eager to please, submission will be no problem for them. But if God has given you strong-willed children, you can expect major battles as they attempt to see how much— and how often—they can get their own way. But God's command doesn't suddenly become just good advice, even though many children continually test the limits to see just how much give there is.

You will often be on your knees in prayer because of a strong-willed, stubborn child, and you will repeatedly ask the Lord to cause your child to yield. You'll also have reason to pray that God will show you new and effective forms of discipline to help your child understand the benefits of obedience.

In training your children to be obedient, you're instilling habits in them that will have a lifelong benefit. The full text of Exodus 20:12 (NIV) is, "Honor your father and your mother, so that you may live long in the land the LORD your God is giving you." In learning to obey their parents, your children are learning to obey God. And God promised the Israelites that if they obeyed Him and kept His commands, He'd bless them and keep them in the Promised Land. If they disobeyed, however, He would cast them out.

May God bless you as you find a balance between prayer and discipline and train up your children in the way they should go. Then when they're old, they will stand a much better chance of not departing from it (Proverbs 22:6).

Dear Father, I understand how difficult it can be to yield to Your will, because sometimes I too struggle to surrender what I want to do. Make me more obedient to You so that I in turn can require obedience from my children. Help them, Lord, not to be stubborn and willful but to be yielded to Your Spirit in all areas. God, if this is to be a contest of wills between me and a strong-willed child, help me not to weaken but to be strong in You. In Jesus' name. Amen.

FOR FURTHER THOUGHT

- Was it always easy for Jesus to yield to His Father's will?
- What does "Your will be done" usually mean for kids? To whom do they yield?
- What is many children's least favorite verse in the New Testament? Why?

63.

PRAYING TO FORGIVE

Children quarrel, hold grudges, and seek revenge just like adults do. And like adults, children need to forgive. You might hear people say, "Oh, don't worry. Children are so forgiving." Sometimes this is true of very young children, but older children and teens often struggle to overlook offenses and let them go.

Jesus said, "Love your enemies! Pray for those who persecute you!" (Matthew 5:44 NLT). Since Jesus has advised us to pray for those who hate and harm us, it comes as no surprise to learn that He prayed for God to forgive those who were crucifying Him. "When they came to the place called The Skull, there they crucified Him and the criminals, one on the right and the other on the left. But Jesus was saying, 'Father, forgive them; for they do not know what they are doing' " (Luke 23:33–34 NASB).

You may be tempted to think that Jesus could forgive only because He was the perfect Son of God and He knew, after all, that it was His Father's will that He die on the cross. If so, you might assume that you'll be excused for *not* loving your enemies or forgiving them. But in truth Jesus gave a command and then set an example for you to follow.

Forgiveness is not an option, a higher calling for only the most dedicated saints. It's the very heart of Jesus' message, and every Christian can and should practice it. Your children also need to forgive those who offend them. Forgiveness brings peace and healing to their souls; it draws them close to God's heart and ensures that they will be forgiven as well. The reverse is also true. Jesus said, "If you do not forgive others their sins, your Father will not forgive your sins" (Matthew 6:15 NIV).

The best way to teach these principles to your children is first of all to believe them and put them into action in your own life—so your children can learn by your example. This may or may not come easily to you. If it doesn't, then before praying for your children to practice forgiveness, you need to pray for God to work in your own heart. It's difficult enough to find opportunities to teach biblical truths that you believe your kids *must* learn. But it's nearly impossible to teach things that you don't feel are relevant or important.

Ephesians 4:32 (NKJV) says, "Be kind to one another, tenderhearted, forgiving one another, even as God in Christ forgave you." Women, even Christian women, too often hold on to offenses and never truly forgive the offender. They can accept the need to be polite to others simply because it shows good manners. Women can be kind—especially in public—even if it's just an act and they're actually seething with resentment inside. But it's very difficult to fake being tenderhearted. God Himself is tenderhearted toward us, and we are to strive to be like Him.

If you live out these principles of true forgiveness and your children have repeated occasions to see you forgive someone who has wronged you, they'll readily learn from your example.

Father in heaven, help me to be kind. Let my heart
be tender so that I will have compassion on others
and forgive them. And please fill my children's hearts

with the same kindness, tenderness, and compassion.
Help them to fully grasp why it's so important to
forgive others. Help them never to seek to strike out
in revenge, even during times when it's necessary
to seek justice or right a wrong. Give me the wisdom
and love I need to guide them in these matters.
In Jesus' name I pray. Amen.

FOR FURTHER THOUGHT

- Why is it difficult for children to forgive those who offend them?

- How important is it for Christians to forgive? Is it merely optional?

- How does forgiveness benefit the person doing the forgiving?

- Why is being tenderhearted so important to forgiveness?

64.

WHAT SHALL I DO, LORD?

After Stephen's death, Saul went to the high priest and asked for letters of authorization to arrest Christians in Damascus and bring them in chains to Jerusalem. But as he was approaching Damascus, a bright light flashed around him, and he fell to the ground. Then, as he lay in the dust, he heard a voice asking, "Saul, Saul, why are you persecuting Me? It is hard for you to kick against the goads" (Acts 26:14 NASB). Jesus was convicting Saul like a farmer prodding an ox with a goad, but Saul, like a stubborn ox, was kicking back.

Saul asked, "Who are You, Lord?"

He said, "I am Jesus whom you are persecuting" (Acts 9:4–5 NASB).

Saul asked, "What shall I do, Lord?"

Jesus said, "Get up and go on into Damascus, and there you will be told of all that has been appointed for you to do" (Acts 22:10 NASB).

Then Jesus added, "For this purpose I have appeared to you, to appoint you a minister and a witness not only to the things which you have seen, but also to the things in which I will appear to you. . .to open their eyes so that they may turn from darkness to light and from the dominion of Satan to God, that they may receive forgiveness of sins and an inheritance among those who have been sanctified by faith in Me" (26:16–18 NASB).

Saul saw and heard Jesus in all His heavenly glory and called Him "Lord." He instantly became submissive and prayed, "What shall I do, Lord?"

When God wanted to get through to Saul, He appeared in human form in a brilliant flash of light. *And* He made Saul blind. And to make sure Saul got the message, He spoke actual words. However, the men traveling with Saul heard the sound of a voice but couldn't make out any words. They saw the light but couldn't distinguish a form. If Saul had seen and heard only what they had, he would've been left guessing who was speaking and what was being said.

Much of the time, God seems to speak to believers today in just such a muffled tone, or to use actions without explanations. It can be difficult to know what He's saying. You may have a traffic accident. Or you may get a huge, unexpected bill. Or you may get sick. God often allows such things to get your attention, and He usually has a specific message He's trying to get across. But what *is* it?

It's difficult enough for adults to interpret God's sign language, and children definitely need help making sense of these showstoppers. That's when you need to come alongside your child and ask, "Have you prayed about what God is trying to tell you?" Then gently ask questions like, "Do you think He might be telling you to slow down to avoid accidents?"

At the same time, it's important to avoid becoming hyperspiritual, reading imaginary messages into everyday incidents. Your children will tire of such "lessons" very quickly. You yourself dislike when well-meaning friends do it to you, right?

The truth is, God often does speak to believers today— both adults and children. He speaks to their consciences, convicting them to do or not do something. . .but they dismiss it as their own thoughts. He speaks to them with a Bible verse that pinpoints an issue in their lives. . .but they brush it away like an annoying mosquito. So then God reverts to sign language.

He says, "As many as I love, I rebuke and chasten" (Revelation 3:19 NKJV). First God rebukes you, but if you or your children turn a deaf ear to His rebuke, He gets out the rod and prepares to chasten you. You ignore *that* at your peril.

> *Dear Lord, I thank You for speaking to me and my children, whether clearly or through symbolic actions. I thank You also for Your loving rebukes and chastisements, which are proof of Your love, hard though they may be to accept at times. Give me wisdom when I help my children to interpret the messages You're sending them. I pray that they'll be sensitive to Your Spirit and quickly understand what You're trying to say. In Jesus' name. Amen.*

FOR FURTHER THOUGHT

- Why do you think God didn't give a clear message to Paul's companions?
- Why does God so often use sign language with believers today?
- What's the difference between the Lord's rebuke and His chastening?

65.

PRAYERS RISING AS A MEMORIAL

Maybe you've been discouraged after praying repeatedly for a situation but seeing no change take place. You may wonder, "What's the matter, Lord? Didn't You promise in Your Word, 'Call unto me, and I will answer thee,' and 'If ye shall ask any thing in my name I will do it'?" (Jeremiah 33:3; John 14:14 KJV).

Of course, you realize there are conditions to God's answering of prayer: (a) you have to ask in faith (Mark 11:24); (b) your request has to be within His will (1 John 5:14–15); and (c) you have to be obedient to Him (1 John 3:22). But it's perplexing when you're doing your best to meet all these conditions and the Lord still hasn't answered your prayers. Often the reason is that there's a *set time* for Him to answer, and all the necessary conditions have to be in place. This principle is illustrated by the following story.

At Caesarea there was a Roman soldier named Cornelius, a centurion in the Italian Regiment. He and all his family were devout and God-fearing, and he gave generously to those in need and prayed regularly. One day at about 3:00 p.m. he had a vision. A holy angel appeared before him and said, "Cornelius!" Trembling, Cornelius asked, "What is it, Lord?"

The angel answered, "Your prayers and gifts to the poor have come up as a memorial offering before God. Now send men to Joppa to bring back a man named Simon who is called Peter. . . . He will bring you a message through which you and all your household will be saved." After the angel vanished, Cornelius called two of his servants and a soldier and sent them to find Peter (Acts 10:1–8; 11:14 NIV).

What does it mean for prayers to "come up as a memorial offering"? Well, in the Old Testament, a memorial offering was a handful of fine flour and oil with frankincense (incense). The priest burned it "as a memorial on the altar, an offering made by fire, a sweet aroma to the LORD" (Leviticus 2:2 NKJV). And in the book of Revelation we read, "Another angel. . .was given much incense to offer, with the prayers of all God's people, on the golden altar in front of the throne. The smoke of the incense, together with the prayers of God's people, went up before God from the angel's hand" (Revelation 8:3–4 NIV).

This is what the angel meant when he told Cornelius, "Your prayers. . .have come up as a memorial offering before God." Cornelius had prayed regularly, but like many Christians today, he had little indication that he'd been heard. But at the right time, a time set by God, He acknowledged and answered Cornelius.

You may pray for your children often, but there seems to be no answer. You may think your prayers go unheard, but that's simply not true: God hears them all as you pray them, and at a set time He considers them all. . .and sends the answer.

In heaven, John saw "the souls of those who had been slain because of the word of God and the testimony they had maintained. They called out in a loud voice, 'How long, Sovereign Lord, holy and true, until you judge the inhabitants of the earth and avenge our blood?' Then each of them was given a white robe, and they were told to *wait a little longer*, until the full number of their fellow servants, their brothers and sisters, were killed just as they had been" (Revelation 6:9–11 NIV, emphasis added).

When you see your daughter going astray, you're impatient for her to get back on the right path as soon as possible. Or if your son needs to learn an important lesson, you have trouble understanding why this must take time. You don't want to "wait a little longer." But keep praying, and at the right time, in God's time, your prayers will be answered.

Heavenly Father, I confess I grow impatient waiting for certain prayers to be answered. I want my children to grow up and change. . .right now. I realize it takes time—years, in fact—for them to develop and mature physically and mentally, but for some reason I've expected spiritual changes to happen more rapidly. Please give me patience and help me to trust that You're working in their lives, even when it seems that nothing is happening. In Jesus' name. Amen.

FOR FURTHER THOUGHT

- Why do you think God often has specific, set times to answer prayer?
- How does waiting on Him teach you trust, patience, and persistence?
- When you think God is ignoring you, what might actually be happening?

66.

PRAYING WHEN YOU'RE UNCERTAIN

Down through the years, you'll have occasion to pray frequently for your children—for behavioral issues, recovery from sickness, protection, salvation, a close walk with God, and wisdom to make good choices. And you may wonder just how certain you can be that God will answer your prayers.

Some believers present *all* their petitions tentatively, subject to God's approval. They base this approach on Jesus' prayer, "If it is possible, may this cup be taken from me. Yet not as I will, but as you will" (Matthew 26:39 NIV). They submit prayer requests, not demands. Other people, however, are very definite when they pray. They state exactly what they want, insist upon it, and inform God that they're counting it as done—because Jesus said, "Whatever you ask for in prayer, believe that you have received it, and it will be yours" (Mark 11:24 NIV).

Which approach is right? It's helpful to study the prayers of the early Christians, who had personally heard Jesus teach on the subject.

One day King Herod arrested Peter and James. He had James killed and was planning to execute Peter. "Peter was therefore kept in prison, but constant prayer was offered to God for him by the church" (Acts 12:5 NKJV). (The New American Standard Bible says, "Prayer for him was being made *fervently* by the church," and the New International Version says, "The church was *earnestly* praying to God for him.")

Then, in the middle of the night, in direct answer to those many prayers, an angel appeared, broke open Peter's chains, and unlocked the prison doors—all while keeping the guards sound asleep. Peter escaped and "came to the house of Mary, the mother of John whose surname was Mark, where many were gathered together praying" (Acts 12:12 NKJV).

Peter knocked at the gate, and a servant girl came out. When she recognized his voice, she was so giddy with joy that she didn't open the gate but rather flew into the house and announced that Peter was outside! Remember, they had been praying fervently for his release. But they told her, "You are beside yourself!" When she insisted that it *was* Peter, they argued, "It is his angel" (v. 15 NKJV). They knew good and well that Peter couldn't be at the gate. After all, he was locked up in prison.

Peter, meanwhile, continued quietly knocking. "And when they opened the door and saw him, they were astonished" (v. 16 NKJV). So when they were praying for Peter to be set free, were they claiming, "Believe that you have received it" (Mark 11:24 NIV)? Apparently not. Yet you have to wonder why they were so surprised. After all, God had done this exact same miracle—for all twelve apostles—a few years earlier (Acts 5:17–19).

So which of the two prayer approaches is right? They both are, depending on the circumstances and God's will. When you *know* God's will for your children, you can pray with confidence (see 1 John 5:14–15). But when you don't know with certainty if something is His will, then you must pray that if it *is* His will, or *within* His overall will, He will do it. And you should pray fervently and earnestly like the early Christians did.

Most likely, they had the former angelic jailbreak in mind, and that gave them faith that God could do such a miracle again—which is why they had faith to pray at all. But did they know for certain God *would* do such a miracle again? No, they didn't. Their surprise that He did the miracle wasn't due to lack of faith but simply to a lack of knowledge regarding His precise will.

When you don't know God's will for your children in a specific circumstance, that's all the more reason to pray fervently and earnestly.

Father in heaven, I have faith in Your power and Your promises, but much of the time I don't know what Your will is for my children in a given situation. I may assume that I know what Your will is, but I've been mistaken in the past and, as a result, have become disappointed in You for "not keeping Your promises." Forgive me, Lord. I'm trying the best I know how. I ask You to give me more faith when I pray, as well as wisdom and a fervent spirit. In Jesus' name I pray. Amen.

FOR FURTHER THOUGHT

- How much do the Jerusalem Christians' prayers remind you of *your* prayers?

- Did their surprise at Peter's arrival show a lack of faith? Why do you think that?

- How should you pray for your kids when you don't know what God's will is?

67.

PRAYERS FOR PROTECTION

Paul was in danger frequently, but God was with him and even warned him what would happen. For example, in Corinth the Lord said to Paul, "Do not be afraid; keep on speaking, do not be silent. For I am with you, and no one is going to attack and harm you" (Acts 18:9–10 NIV). Some months later, there *was* an attack against him, but God made it come to nothing (Acts 18:12–16). He had promised, "No one is going to attack *and* harm you," and though people did attack Paul, they weren't able to harm him.

This is probably why Paul wasn't overly concerned when God began repeatedly warning him that he faced danger in Jerusalem. Paul said, "I am going to Jerusalem, not knowing what will happen to me there. I only know that in every city the Holy Spirit warns me that prison and hardships are facing me" (Acts 20:22–23 NIV).

You may wonder why, if the Spirit warned him that prison and hardships awaited him, Paul said in the same breath that he didn't know *what* would happen there. Well, he obviously was expecting protection from the potential threat just like he'd experienced in Corinth. Nevertheless, he knew the threat was serious and very real, so he wrote to fellow believers, "I beg you. . .that you strive together with me in prayers to God for me, that I may be delivered from those in Judea who do not believe" (Romans 15:30–31 NKJV). His hope, obviously, was that he'd be *delivered* from those looming dangers.

To other Christians, he wrote, "On [God] we have set our hope that he will continue to deliver us, as you help us by your prayers. Then many will give thanks. . .for the gracious favor granted us in answer to the prayers of many" (2 Corinthians 1:10–11 NIV).

Paul knew the situation was fluid and could go one way or another, which is why he often requested prayer for protection. The same is true of your children today. They may not have mortal enemies like Paul had, but they will benefit greatly from protection against accidents and illness.

The Bible promises, "The angel of the LORD encamps around those who fear Him, and rescues them" (Psalm 34:7 NASB). Many people have idyllic pictures in their minds of angels with great white wings doting over small children. They assume that *all* children are protected. Obviously, they haven't watched the evening news recently. Angels don't automatically protect anyone; you need to pray that God sends them to guard your children.

Many parents have testified that they were going about their day when they received a distinct impression that their children were in danger and they needed to pray for them immediately. They obeyed the summons, only to find out later that their son or daughter had been spared a serious accident. God *can* protect your children, He *can* warn you when they're in danger, but He still needs you to pray. This shows the vital importance of prayer.

And you can't stop praying for your children when they enter their teen years. That's precisely the time they get their driver's license, become more daring, often refuse to listen to advice to be careful, and frequently have the idea that they're indestructible. This is about the same time that many parents' hair begins turning gray. So you definitely need to continue praying for your children then.

Dear Lord, thank You that You put Your angels around my children to protect them. But help me not to neglect to pray for them. An awful lot depends on my concern and my prayers. Protect my children from physical accidents. Protect them from bullies at school, in the neighborhood, and on the internet. Protect them from disease. Protect them from being wounded emotionally. Protect them from deceivers and enemies of the faith. In Jesus' name I pray. Amen.

FOR FURTHER THOUGHT

- Why do parents often not bother to pray for their children's safety?
- Since you know accidents can easily happen, why wouldn't you pray?
- Has God ever done a miracle when you prayed for your kids' protection?

68.

A MOTHER'S UNCEASING PRAYERS

Paul was a spiritual parent to many. He wrote to the Christians of Corinth, "Even if you had ten thousand others to teach you about Christ, you have only one spiritual father. For I became your father in Christ Jesus when I preached the Good News to you" (1 Corinthians 4:15 NLT). After Paul led people to faith in Christ, like a true father, he cared for them, nurtured them in the faith, and—very importantly—prayed for them.

Paul continued to pray for them years later, even when he was distant. He wrote to Philemon, "I thank my God, making mention of you always in my prayers" (Philemon 1:4 NKJV). He wrote to Timothy, "Without ceasing I remember you in my prayers night and day" (2 Timothy 1:3 NKJV), and he assured the Christians of Colosse, "We. . .do not cease to pray for you" (Colossians 1:9 NKJV).

Paul longed to be with them personally, to teach them, pray with them, and strengthen their faith—and to this end he prayed that God would make a way for him to travel to them. He wrote to the Christians of Rome, "For God. . .is my witness as to how *unceasingly* I make mention of you, *always* in my prayers making request, if perhaps now at last by the will of God I may succeed in coming to you" (Romans 1:9–10 NASB, emphasis added). You get the impression that Paul prayed for fellow believers a *lot*.

He also prayed to travel to Thessalonica, telling the believers there, "We give thanks to God always for you all, making mention of you in our prayers. . .night and day praying exceedingly that we might see your face" (1 Thessalonians 1:2; 3:10 KJV). But, as Paul explained, the devil relentlessly hindered his travel plans. "We wanted to come to you—certainly I, Paul, did, again and again—but Satan blocked our way" (1 Thessalonians 2:18 NIV).

These verses not only show how frequently and how persistently Paul prayed but also reveal *why* he had to pray so much: "The devil walks about like a roaring lion, seeking whom he may devour" (1 Peter 5:8 NKJV). Because Satan was fighting God's will, Paul had to stand his ground and fight the good fight of faith, day after day. He couldn't just let things slide and hope everything turned out okay. He had to be militant.

Paul was constantly checking up on those he had led to Christ. He wrote, "For this reason, when I could no longer endure it, I sent to know your faith, lest by some means the tempter had tempted you, and our labor might be in vain" (1 Thessalonians 3:5 NKJV). This is also why you, as a parent, must never cease praying for your children. The same cruel, relentless tempter who tried to destroy the faith of the first Christians is still in the world today and would love to destroy your children's faith. This thought ought to motivate you to pray.

Depending on your circumstances or the stage of life you are in, you may have to spend much of your day away from your children. But whatever your situation, you can always pray. You may not have prayed much up until now, but God can transform you into a woman of prayer and, as a result, transform your children's lives as well. Sometimes you might feel that your prayers aren't accomplishing much, that you can't devote enough time to prayer to make a real difference, but let God be the judge of that. He calls you to pray. It's up to Him to answer.

> *Dear God, please help me to be persistent in watching over my children's faith. Help me to be faithful to love them, teach them, and pray with them when I'm with them—and to pray for them when we're apart. May I never give in to fear, for You are much greater than the enemy. Nevertheless, I know that he doesn't stop fighting, so help me to be just as relentless—in fact, more so. Help me to be a warrior for the faith. I trust You to strengthen and keep my children. . .but help me to pray. In Jesus' name I ask. Amen.*

FOR FURTHER THOUGHT

- Why is it important not to take your children's faith for granted?
- What is one of the main reasons parents need to pray?
- What was Paul's goal? What was Satan's goal? What is your goal?

69.

TEACHING CHILDREN TO PRAY

When Paul and his companions were sailing to Jerusalem, they stopped at the port city of Tyre for seven days and fellowshipped with the local church. Luke wrote, "When we returned to the ship at the end of the week, the entire congregation, including women and children, left the city and came down to the shore with us. There we knelt, prayed, and said our farewells" (Acts 21:5–6 NLT).

From this passage, we see that the first Christians didn't hesitate to include their children in public prayer. It was natural for them, and children learned how to pray by doing so with their families and their church.

Public prayer was a part of life in the Old Testament as well, both in serious and in happy times. "While Ezra was praying, and while he was confessing, weeping, and bowing down. . .a very large assembly of men, women, and children gathered to him from Israel; for the people wept" (Ezra 10:1 NKJV). On a separate occasion, the Jews "offered great sacrifices, and rejoiced, for God had made them rejoice with great joy; the women and the children also rejoiced" (Nehemiah 12:43 NKJV).

It's important to pray *for* your children, but if they're to develop fully in their relationship with God, you also must teach them how to pray themselves. Prayer is an essential life skill. It might not occur to you that they don't know where to start or what to say, but remember, even Jesus' disciples had to be taught. "Now it came to pass, as He was praying in a certain place, when He ceased, that one of His disciples said to Him, 'Lord, teach us to pray, as John also taught his disciples' " (Luke 11:1 NKJV).

This verse shows us two things: First, Jesus sometimes prayed openly so that His disciples could *see* and *hear* Him. Other times He prayed in private. In contrast to the hypocritical public prayers of the Pharisees, Jesus taught, "When you pray, go into your inner room, close your door and pray to your Father who is in secret" (Matthew 6:6 NASB). Jesus Himself frequently went to a "solitary place" to pray (Mark 1:35 KJV). Consequently, some people think that public prayers are unscriptural or not as effective as private prayers.

But there's a time and a place for everything. In the days of King Jehoshaphat, three nations invaded Judah. Jehoshaphat proclaimed a fast, people gathered from all over Judah to seek the Lord, and Jehoshaphat stood in the temple court and prayed publicly (2 Chronicles 20:6–12). And after Jesus' ascension, 120 of His disciples prayed together in one large upper room for ten days (Acts 1:12–15).

The second thing Luke 11:1 shows us is that although Jesus' disciples had just finished listening to Him pray, they still felt the need to ask for pointers on how best to do it. In other words, "Teach us to pray like *that*!" They wanted Jesus to explain it and break it down for them, just as John the Baptist had done for his disciples.

Perhaps you're in the habit of reading a devotional after dinner and then engaging in family prayer. Or perhaps you pray with your children after a Bible story at bedtime. But whenever you do it, it's important to intentionally teach your children how to pray, not only by letting them hear you pray but by guiding them in their own prayers.

Remind them of things they should pray for. Remind them to come before the Lord with a trusting attitude. Remind them to give thanks to Him. Remind them to quote promises from the Bible when they pray.

You can model a prayerful attitude throughout the day as well. For example, if one of your children complains to you about a problem they're facing, you can stop right then and there and pray with them about it.

Father in heaven, I pray that You help me teach my children how to communicate with You so that it comes naturally to them when they're older. Help me to model dependence on You so they can see how important it is to seek Your face. Let my prayers be reverent, spontaneous, and sincere—never stilted or empty. Help me to be consistent and intentional in teaching my children to pray. In Jesus' name. Amen.

FOR FURTHER THOUGHT

- When and how often do you pray with your whole family?
- What can you do to teach your children the nuts and bolts of prayer?
- Why is it important to teach your children how to pray?

70.

LABORING EARNESTLY IN PRAYER

For many moms, the idea of praying for their children for fifteen minutes doesn't just seem boring but seems like very hard work, impossible to fit into an already busy day. And they're exhausted just thinking about praying for half an hour or a full hour. The fact is, putting your whole heart into prayer can take a lot out of you and your schedule.

When Jesus was in the Garden of Gethsemane, "being in agony, He prayed more earnestly. Then His sweat became like great drops of blood falling down to the ground" (Luke 22:44 NKJV). Praying *that* fervently is called for only on rare occasions. Jesus prayed that way because He was about to be crucified.

When you hear about Christians who spend an hour praying every day, you might think, *Those people must have some serious time on their hands!* You may feel you're too busy to pray more than five minutes a day—ten minutes at the very most. If you can't spare an hour, you can't. Do what you can.

But for two thousand years, Christians have been moved by Jesus' question. He had asked His disciples to pray with Him, but they fell asleep. So Jesus asked, "Couldn't you men keep watch with me for one hour?" (Matthew 26:40 NIV). The implication is that praying for an hour wasn't too much to ask. But the amount of time spent praying isn't the main issue. What's important is praying wholeheartedly.

Paul wrote to the church in Colosse: "Epaphras, who

is one of your number. . .[is] always laboring earnestly for you in his prayers, that you may stand perfect and fully assured in all the will of God. For I testify for him that he has a deep concern for you" (Colossians 4:12–13 NASB). That's the secret: if you have a *deep concern* for your children, spending time praying for them comes much more easily.

The New International Version renders this passage: "He is always wrestling in prayer for you, that you may stand firm in all the will of God, mature and fully assured." Epaphras didn't exert himself only once in serious prayer; he kept wrestling in prayer day after day, month after month. He wasn't just interested in his fellow Christians making it through one emergency; his goal was to see them solidly established and standing firm in God's will, able to weather all the storms of life.

That should be your goal with your children as well. You may think you only need to exert yourself in prayer anytime your kids go through a period of special testing. Yes, you should pray for them then, but in truth you need to pray for them constantly. And though some intense crises last for only a few hours, others—though somewhat less intense—can drag on for weeks or months.

Paul wrote, "Pray without ceasing" (1 Thessalonians 5:17 KJV). Elsewhere he urged, "Pray in the Spirit at all times and on every occasion. Stay alert and be persistent in your prayers for all believers everywhere" (Ephesians 6:18 NLT). You may wonder, *How on earth am I supposed to pray all day long? I have to keep my mind on my work.*

Well, if you obey the great commandment—"Love the Lord your God with all your heart" (Mark 12:30 NIV)—you'll naturally look to God all day long. You'll be thinking about Him and thanking Him for victories and blessings great and small, and you'll automatically commit your concerns to Him as they come up. It may take sustained effort to get in the habit, but after a while you'll find yourself communing with your Father regularly throughout the day.

When your children are going through testings or crises, you may be tempted to worry about them. Don't! Instead, every time a worried thought comes to your mind, turn it into a prayer.

Dear Lord, please forgive me when I shy away from prayer, thinking it's drudgery. Please help me to be genuinely concerned so that prayer comes more naturally to me. And help me to get in the habit of looking to You all day long, continually committing my concerns to You in prayer. In Jesus' name I pray. Amen.

FOR FURTHER THOUGHT

- Why does praying for their children seem like hard work to many parents?
- What are some times when you should labor earnestly in prayer?
- How can you "pray without ceasing" all day long?

71.

THE EPHESIAN BENEDICTION

Paul prayed a powerful prayer for the Christians of Ephesus:

> *For this reason I bow my knees before the Father, from whom every family in heaven and on earth derives its name, that He would grant you, according to the riches of His glory, to be strengthened with power through His Spirit in the inner man, so that Christ may dwell in your hearts through faith; and that you, being rooted and grounded in love, may be able to comprehend with all the saints what is the breadth and length and height and depth, and to know the love of Christ which surpasses knowledge, that you may be filled up to all the fullness of God. Now to Him. . .be the glory in the church and in Christ Jesus to all generations forever and ever. Amen. (Ephesians 3:14–21 NASB)*

First of all, notice that Paul calls God "the Father, from whom every family in heaven and on earth derives its name." We obtain our sense of identity and security through our relationship with Him. "See how very much our Father loves us, for he calls us his children, and that is what we are!" (1 John 3:1 NLT). Moses told the Israelites, "You are the children of the LORD your God" (Deuteronomy 14:1 NKJV). The prophet Hosea added, "You are sons of the living God" (Hosea 1:10 NKJV).

Let's look at the Ephesian benediction closely to see

what Paul prayed for a typical church. Paul often wrote in very long sentences, so let's break things down into bite-size thoughts to see what he was saying. He prayed "that Christ may dwell in your hearts through faith." This is the most vital prayer. When children have the faith to be saved, God then sends the Spirit of His Son into their hearts (see Galatians 4:6).

Paul prayed that the Ephesian believers would be "rooted and grounded in love." Faith without love is empty. Your children must be solidly rooted in love to grow into people who genuinely love others. "When we place our faith in Christ Jesus. . .what is important is faith expressing itself in love," we read in Galatians 5:6 (NLT). To be grounded in love fulfills the two greatest commandments—to love God and to love others (Matthew 22:36–40).

Paul prayed that God "would grant you. . .to be strengthened with power through His Spirit in the inner man." Jesus promised, "You will receive power when the Holy Spirit comes on you" (Acts 1:8 NIV), and your children must continually yield to the Spirit to continue receiving His power (Acts 5:32).

Paul prayed that you may "know the love of Christ which surpasses knowledge." Pray that your children never forget how much Jesus loves them. This awareness will cause them to love Him and serve Him out of gratitude. "We love him, because he first loved us" (1 John 4:19 KJV).

Finally, Paul prayed "that you may be filled up to all the fullness of God." The goal is for your kids to "become mature, attaining to the whole measure of the fullness of Christ" (Ephesians 4:13 NIV).

This is a beautiful prayer to pray often over your

children as they're growing up and making their faith their own. It's vital that they grasp not only correct doctrine and basic Gospel facts but the very heart of what it means to be a Christian. Paul captures it so well in this benediction.

You can nurture a living faith in your children's hearts through word, example, and faithful prayer. And you don't have to be as eloquent as the apostle Paul was in this benediction. Don't even try! Simply pour out your heart to God for your children, and expect Him to hear you and answer you.

Dear God, thank You for being our Father and for causing Your Holy Spirit to dwell in my heart and my children's hearts. Let Your love and gentleness live in them and guide every aspect of their lives. Help them to truly comprehend the love of Christ, the fact that Your Son loved them so much that He died to save them. Help them realize that You truly are their loving heavenly Father who will never leave them. In Jesus' name. Amen.

FOR FURTHER THOUGHT

- Why is ardent love for fellow believers so often stressed in Paul's letters?
- Why do we need to be strengthened with God's power in our spirits?
- In what way does the love of Christ surpass mere knowledge?

About the Authors

JoAnne Simmons dreamed in middle school of someday working in Christian publishing. God blessed that desire and has also given her a fun-loving husband and two precious daughters as the best dream come true.

Ed Strauss was a freelance writer living in British Columbia, Canada, who passed into heaven in 2018. He authored or coauthored more than fifty books for children, tweens, and adults. Ed had a passion for biblical apologetics and, besides writing for Barbour, was published by Zondervan, Tyndale, Moody, and Focus on the Family. Ed had three children: Sharon, Daniel, and Michelle Strauss.

Encouragement Just for Moms!

Encouraging Words for Mothers: Morning and Evening

This 365-day morning and evening devotional book is written *by* a mom—award-winning writer Michelle Medlock Adams—*for* moms. Especially for women with children still at home, it offers brief, relevant, and biblical reflections with monthly themes such as worry, unconditional love, discipline, and prayer, showing how scripture applies to your everyday life.

Flexible Casebound / 978-1-64352-080-3 / $19.99

The Bible Promise Book for Mothers

Motherhood really should come with an operator's manual. The good news is that God's Word provides His insight to some of life's biggest questions. This book provides God's wisdom on dozens of topics—arranged alphabetically—offering hundreds of scripture's most encouraging, hope-filled promises—just for you, Mom!

Hardback / 978-1-64352-310-1 / $15.99